AF540740

WOMEN EDUCATION AND DEVELOPMENT

WOMEN EDUCATION
AND
DEVELOPMENT

Edited by
Dr. Rabi N. Misra

DISCOVERY PUBLISHING HOUSE
NEW DELHI-110002

Published by:
Tilak Wasan
DISCOVERY PUBLISHING HOUSE PVT. LTD.
4383/4B, Ansari Road, Darya Ganj
New Delhi-110 002 (India)
Phone : +91-11-23279245, 23253475, 43596065
E-mail : discoverypublishinghouse@gmail.com
sales@discoverypublishinggroup.com
web : www.discoverypublishinggroup.com

First Edition: **2006**

Reprinted: **2020**

ISBN: 978-81-8356-099-3

Women Education and Development

Printed at:
Infinity Imaging Systems
Delhi

Preface

It is very clear that in India women are performing a lion's share in the growth and development of the nation. If a larger part remains untouched in education, health and socio-economic development, the development of the nation cannot be turned in a progressive manner. A society can be taken as an ideal society if we acknowledge the strength of women in the light of development. If a large chunk remains untouchable, the economic development will be in a regressive manner. In a welfare state like India one can undoubtedly say that education played a vital role in the present juncture of development in India. In the era of globalisation the women are still in the last benches in education, health and socio-economic stages.

Nearly 35 per cent of women are literate in India. They contribute half in population and also have their 1/3rd share in the revenue of the country. But they are only 1 per cent owner in the entire property of the country.

Mahatma Gandhi, Rabindra Nath Tagore and other eminent leaders in India are expressed their view for women education. In spite of this and after six decades of independence we are still in stagnant in education. A mother who is the first teacher of the child and who manages the home is now not regarded in the progress of the state. In the light of this, the women education is very secret in the success of every respect of the country. So this book has taken an attempt in collecting various articles from the eminent writers which will throw a good light to the darken side. This book will no doubt be helpful to all the categories of the people, organisations and Government as a whole.

Dr. R.N. Misra

Acknowledgement

I am very much thankful to all paper contributors of this book, it is not possible on my part to edit this book without their kind help and co-operation.

I am also thankful to Mr. Pinaki Mohanty, Lecturer in English, Ramanarayan College, Dura-10, Ganjam (Orissa) for his kind help and cooperation in editing this book.

I am also thankful to my wife Swarna Prava who has cooperated me for all the time for editing this book. I am also thankful to my two sons.

I am very much thankful and grateful to Sri Tilak Wasan, Proprietor, Discovery Publishing House, New Delhi who had readily accepted my proposal in publishing this book in spite of his heavy pressure during this session. I, on behalf of all paper contributors, family members, and friends very much thankful to all staff members of Discovery Publishing House for their kind help and co-operation provided by them in publishing this book in time.

Dr. Rabi N. Misra

List of Contributors

Prof. (Dr.) R.P. Sharma a retired professor of Economics, Berhampur University, Bhanja Bihar, Orissa, retired from his service in the year 1996. He has produced eight Ph.D. Scholars. He is a writer of four books and published a number of articles in different journals. At present he is the Director, Institute of Economics Studies, Berhampur–10 (Ganjam) Orissa.

Mr. Devadutta Choudhury is a Reader in Economics and working at B.P. Mahavidyalaya, Samantiapalli, Berhampur (Gm.) Mr. Choudhury has published a number of articles in different journals. He is also associated with various voluntary organisations.

Dr. Anil Kumar Sahu was born in the year 1960. He has done his M.Com., M.B.A., and Ph.D. in Management from Berhampur University, Bhanja Bihar (Orissa). Now Dr. Sahu is working as a Reader in MBA, Berhampur University (Orissa). He now guiding four Ph.D. Scholars and published three articles in different journals.

Dr. Satya Narayan Pathi was born in the year 1961. He has done his M.Com. and M.Phil from Berhampur University, Bhanja Bihar (Orissa). He has done his Ph.D. from Patna University in the year 1990. Dr. Pathi is now working as a Reader in MBA, Berhampur University (Orissa). He has produced two Ph.D Scholar, and three scholars are doing Ph.D under his guidance.

Dr. Sandhya Rani Das is now working as a faculty member, Department of Economics, Berhampur University, Bhanja Bihar (Orissa) she has published so many articles in different journals.

Mr. Sudhansu Sekhar Nayak was born in the year 1967. He passed M.Com., M.Phil, and LL.B from Berhampur University, Bhanja Bihar (Orissa). Now Mr. Nayak is working as a Lecturer in Commerce, Ramanarayan College, Dura–10, Ganjam (Affiliated to Berhampur University, Orissa) and doing his Ph.D. under the supervision of Dr. R.N. Misra. He has published seven articles in different journals.

Dr. A. Suresh Chandra Patnaik, has done his MBA in the year 1984. He has completed his Ph.D in the year 2004. Dr. Patnaik is working as Reader in MBA Programme of P.G. Centre for Management and Studies, SMIT, Berhampur under Biju Patnaik University of Technology, Orissa. He has published some articles in different journals. He is also a social worker.

Mrs. Babilata Shroff is lecturer in Economics at D.A.V. College, Titilagarh, Orissa. Mrs. Shroff has published more than 12 articles at different journals. She is also engaged in various social activities.

Mr. P.K. Chhotroy, done his M.A. (Economics) in the year 1964. He retired as Principal on 30/11/2003. He has published more than 6 articles in International journals. Now he is engaged in various social activities.

Dr. Kalpana Sahu, is working as a lecturer in Economics at Science College, Hinjilicut, Orissa. She has done her Ph.D in the year 2002. She has published more than 8 articles in different journals.

Dr. Ashok Kumar Panda, a senior lecturer in Commerce at D.A.V. College, Titilagarh, Dist– Bolangeer, Orissa. Dr. Panda got his Ph.D in the year 2003. He has published more than 15 articles in different journals.

Dr. Suresh Kumar Sahu, Senior Faculty, Member, Department of Economics, Science College, Hinjilicut, Orissa. Dr. Sahu has published more than 20 articles in different journals. He is also a good Oriya poet. He is engaged in various social activities.

Contents

1

Role of Women in Managing Small Scale Industrial Units
A Study

Sudhansu Sekhar Nayak*
Dr. Anil Kumar Sahu**
Dr. Rabi N. Misra***

Introduction

The destiny of a nation is moulded and fashioned through its education and in this, the education of women has strategic importance. The significance of the education of women cannot be overemphasised. As per UN Report 1980, Women constitute half of the world population, perform nearly two thirds of work hours, receive one tenth of the world's income and own less than one hundredth per cent of world's property. Half of the India's populations too are women. In the Eight Plan, a shift was made from development to improvement of women. Health, job, income and education are four interdependent variables, which enable a woman to climb high in socio-economic ladder. Female literacy rate in the State has consistently been lower than that of males. Though the female literacy rate in the state increased from 4.5 per cent in 1951 to 50.51 per cent in 2001, it is still lower than the

* Lecturer in Commerce, Ramanarayan College, Dura–10 (Ganjam) Orissa.

** Reader in Dept. of Business Administration, Berhampur University (Ganjam) Orissa.

*** Professor, Dept. of MBA, SMIT, Ankuspur (Gm) Orissa.

national average of 54.16 per cent and also much lower than the male literacy rate of 75.35 per cent in the State. In rural areas, the female literacy rate is 46.66 per cent, which is lower than the state average. Due to this worsening condition, education itself enables a girl to take independent decision in several matters pertaining to her own interest. She can ask for equal treatment in the family and the society, demand for equal rights and protest against any kind of discrimination. Education of the girl child enable her to protest against her early marriage, which is the root cause of her sufferings like ill-health, malnutrition, higher rate of infant mortality and even increased risk to the life of the mother. Due to the lack of proper education, most parents fail to recognise that little mother are not adequately equipped to take care of the newborn child or that early marriage puts tremendous pressure on the girl child to play adult roles quite early in life. Several welfare programmes are being implemented in the state which include setting up of women's training centre, provision of old age pension, rehabilitative services for women in distress, provision of short stay homes for women, etc. Despite various measures taken, the status of women continues to remain backward with gradual spread of education and empowerment, the position of women has begun to change It is the policy of the Government, to bring them into the mainstream.

Scope and Objectives

The present study aims to highlight the role of women in managing Small-Scale Industrial Units in Ganjam District in Orissa State under self-employment scheme known as Prime Minister's Rojagar Yojana (PMRY). The period of the study is limited only to four years i.e. from 2000-01 to 2003-04 and only secondary datas are taken into consideration. The relevant secondary datas are collected from the annual action plan and official records of District Industries Centre (DIC) in Ganjam district. So, all limitations of the secondary data are found in this study.

Progress of Women Education Before Independence

Women education in our country passed through several stages of development. In ancient India, both men and women had an access to education. In the vedic age, equality was given to the women. They enjoyed special opportunity and freedom. Both boys and girls received education in Ashrams and Gurukuls. But in later times education of women was given low priority and the introduction of early marriage acted as a grievous pitfall on the way of education. During the days of the Muslims, the women rotted behind the purdah and were not allowed to mix with men. Due to their economic dependence of men they came to be regarded as the bond slave to men. Some active steps were taken by Government during the year 1902-1917 for the improvement of women education. New plans were devised, separate schools were started, arrangements of conveyance for taking girls to schools were made, inspectresses were appointed, federal prizes were offered to girls and fees were remitted at times, many schools run by local bodies were transferred to government, favourable grants were made to private girls schools, steps were taken to attend ladies to the teaching profession and provincial committees were set up for discussing the problems of girls education. By the end of the year 1947, there were 16,951 institutions reserved for women and the total enrolment of Girls in institutions of all categories was 35,50,503.

Women Education After Independence

After independence several commissions and committees were appointed to suggest measures for the improvement of education in general. University Education commission appointed in 1948-49, recommended for the improvement of women's education at higher education level. The "National Committee on women's Education" was appointed in 1958-59 under the chairmanship of Durgabhai Deshmukh for making a survey of the present system of women's education in 1962 a committee was appointed under the Chairmanship of Hans Meheta to look to the differentiation of curriculum between boys and girls. In the year 1963, Bhaktavatsalam committee was appointed to study the problem of women's education in six states where the education of girls was less developed. The Kothari commission, which has appointed to investigate the problems of education in general, accepted the suggestion of National Committee on Women's Education. In 1968, the Resolution on the National Policy on Education stressed the importance of women education. Since independence, though significant progress has been made in providing facilities for girls and women's education yet the progress is not so encouraging. With the passage of time, the progress of women's education in the development plans has been ensured as a prime focus. Because a social movement requires the revival and creation of necessary atmosphere for the spread of girls education.

Development of Women Under Five Year Plans

Programmes in this sector during the first plan period were mainly welfare oriented. The Central Social Welfare Board (CSWB) was established by the Government of India in 1953 to take up nation-wide welfare measures for the development of women and children. During the second plan period, women were organised into Mahila Mandals in rural areas for facilitating convergence of health, nutrition and welfare measures. The Third and Fourth plans accorded high priority to women's education, immunization of pre-school children and supplementary diet for children and expectant and nursing mothers. In the Fifth plan, there was a shift in emphasis from welfare orientation to a developmental approach with the objective of removal of poverty and attainment of self reliance. In the Sixth Plan, a variety of programmes and schemes were taken up for improving working conditions of women and to raise their socio-economic status. Vocational training centres were set up for developing their skills. Non-formal education centres were set up exclusively for girls. Women were assisted through IRDP, TRYSEM and DWCRA. During the Seventh Plan period, several beneficiary oriental programmes were launched for providing direct benefit with the objective of raising the economic and social status of the target group of women. In the Eighth Plan a shift was made from development to empowerment of women and a number of measures were undertaken for their social and economic emancipation. The empowerment measures for women included the constitutional amendment for at least 30 per cent representation in all elected local self government bodies such as Panchayati Raj Institutions of Municipalities, establishment of a National Commission for Women at the centre and State Commissions for Women at the state level and launching of Mahila Samrudhi Yojana (MSY) for sensitising women at grassroot level in the rural area. During the Ninth Plan period, important components for the strategy proposal to be adopted for development of women are as follows:

(a) Women's education and eradication illiteracy among girls will be given high priority.

(b) Efforts will be made to improve their skills and capacity to earn by way of providing vocational training in various fields.

(c) Steps will be taken for projecting a positive image of girls and women.

In the Tenth Plan, four more strategies have been added in addition to the above.

(a) To improve the nutritional and health status of children below the age of six years.

(b) To reduce the incidence of infant and child mortality and malnutrition.

(c) To ensure that funds/benefits are earmarked for women in all women related sectors.

(d) Inclusion of an identifiable women component plan in programmes of all sectors of development to sure that the benefits reach the women.

Analysis

The women beneficiaries who were applied for establishment of SSI units under PMRY scheme in the district are categorised into five groups according to their educational qualification. They are below matriculation class, up to matriculation class, upto +2 class, up to graduation class and up to Post-graduation class. The analysis of the data is made under three heads:

1. Educational qualification-wise progress under PMRY scheme in women beneficiaries.
2. Educational qualification-wise defaulters in women beneficiaries under PMRY scheme.
3. Educational qualification-wise sickness in women beneficiaries under PMRY scheme.

1. ***Qualification-wise progress under PMRY scheme in women beneficiaries:*** The qualification-wise sanction and disbursement of PMRY loan for women beneficiaries in the district are shown in Table—1.1.

Table 1.1: Qualification-wise Progress Under PMRY Scheme in Women Beneficiaries

Sl. No.	*Educational Qualification*	*2000-2001*			*2001-2002*			*2002-2003*			*2003-2004*			*Total*		
		S No.	*D No.*	*%*	*S No.*	*D No.*	*%*	*S No.*	*D No.*	*%*	*S No.*	*D No.*	*%*	*S*	*D*	*%*
1.	Below Matriculation	12	06	50%	06	04	66.6%	11	06	54.5%	12	07	53.8%	42	23	54.7%
2.	Upto Matriculation	15	08	53.3%	07	05	71.4%	10	08	80%	11	08	72.7%	43	29	67.4%
3.	Upto +2 class	17	09	52.9%	09	06	66.6%	13	08	61.5%	12	09	75%	51	32	62.7%
4.	Upto graduation class	20	12	60%	08	07	87.5%	10	09	90%	11	09	81.8%	49	37	75.5%
5.	Post-graduation class	22	16	72.2%	10	08	80%	12	10	83.3%	14	12	85.7%	58	40	79.3%
	Total	**86**	**51**	**59.3%**	**40**	**30**	**75%**	**56**	**41**	**73.2%**	**61**	**45**	**73.7%**	**243**	**167**	**68.7%**

Source: Annual Action Plan, 2003-04, PMRY, DIC, Ganjam. (Orissa).

S = Sanction, D= Disbursement, P= Percentage.

Table–1.1 shows that during these four yours, 243 number of cases of women beneficiaries were sanctioned by the banks but only 167 number of cases were disbursed for payment of loan which accounts for 68.7 per cent. In this period, the highest sanction is made to the women having P.G. qualification which constituted 79.3 per cent followed by graduation qualification which 75.5 per cent and lowest sanction is made to the women having below matriculation qualification which constituted 54.7 per cent.

2. ***Qualification-wise defaulters in women beneficiaries:*** The qualification-wise borrowers and defaulters in PMRY loan for women beneficiaries in the district are explained in Table—1.2.

Table 1.2: Qualification-wise Defaulter in Women Beneficiaries Under P.M.R.Y. Scheme

Sl. No.	*Educational Qualification*	*2000-01*			*2001-02*			*2002-03*			*2003-04*			*Total*		
		B No.	*D No.*	*P*	*B No.*	*D No.*	*P*	*B No.*	*D No.*	*P*	*B No.*	*D No.*	*P*	*B No.*	*D No.*	*P*
1.	Below Matriculation	13	02	15.3%	07	01	14.2%	11	02	18.1%	40	06	15%	40	06	15%
2.	Upto Matriculation	12	03	25.0%	06	02	33.3%	08	02	25.0%	09	02	33.3%	35	10	28.5%
3.	Upto +2 class	09	04	44.4%	08	03	37.5%	10	04	40%	10	04	40%	37	15	40.5%
4.	Upto Graduation Class	08	05	62.5%	05	04	80%	07	05	71.4%	08	06	75%	28	20	71.4%
5.	Post Graduation Class	09	07	77.7%	04	04	100%	07	05	71.4%	07	06	85.7%	27	22	81.4%
	Total	**52**	**21**	**41.1%**	**30**	**14**	**46.6%**	**41**	**17**	**41.4%**	**45**	**21**	**46.6%**	**167**	**73**	**43.7%**

Source: Annual Action Plan, 2003-04, PMRY, DIC, Ganjam (Orissa)

B = Borrowers, D = Defaulters, C = Percentage.

Table–1.2 shows that out of 167 women borrowers, 73 borrowers are defaulter in payment of bank loan which accounts for 43.7 per cent during these four years. In this period, the maximum defaulter was in the qualification of P.G. level which constituted 81.4 per cent followed by graduation level which was 71.4 per cent and minimum defaulter was in the qualification of below matriculation which was only 15 per cent.

3. ***Qualification-wise sickness in women beneficiaries:*** The qualification-wise sick units established by women beneficiaries in the district under PMRY scheme are explained in Table—1.3.

Table 1.3: Qualification-wise Sick Units Established by Women Beneficiaries Under P.M.R.Y. Scheme

Sl. No.	*Educational Qualifications*	*2000-2001*			*2001-02*			*2002-03*			*2003-04*			*Total*		
		G	*S*	*P*	*G*	*S*	*P*	*G*	*S*	*P*	*G*	*S*	*P*	*G*	*S*	*P*
1.	Below Matriculation	09	01	11.1%	05	–	–	07	–	–	08	–	–	29	01	3.4%
2.	Upto Matriculation	08	01	12.5%	06	–	–	06	–	–	07	–	–	27	01	3.7%
3.	Upto +2 Class	10	02	20%	04	01	25%	08	–	–	09	–	–	31	03	9.6%
4.	Upto Graduation Class	11	02	18.1%	05	02	40%	07	01	14.2%	06	–	–	29	05	17.2%
5.	Post Graduation Class	10	03	30%	07	02	28.5%	11	02	18.1%	12	02	16.6%	40	09	22.5%
	Total	**48**	**09**	**18.7%**	**27**	**05**	**18.5%**	**39**	**03**	**7.65**	**42**	**02**	**4.7%**	**156**	**19**	**12.1%**

Source: Annual Action Plan, 2003-04, PMRY, DIC, Ganjam. (Orissa)

G = Units Grounded, S = Sick units, P = Percentage.

Table—1.3 shows that during the four years, 156 SSI units were established by the women beneficiaries in the district of this, 19 SSI units were found sick which accounts for only 12.1 per cent. The sick units were higher in case of P.G. qualification borrowers which constituted 22.5 per cent followed by graduation level borrowers which constituted 17.2 per cent and lower in case of below matriculation borrowers which was 3.4 per cent.

Suggestions

Various measures have been suggested for the improvement of women's education and development. These measures are:

1. Effective enforcement of compulsory/vocational education and creation of social climate among the village community to enroll all girls of school going age.
2. Encouraging married women to take up at least part time teaching in village schools and to work as school mother and provision of special incentive to teachers.
3. Initiating action and participating in educative propaganda to break down traditional prejudices against girl's education.
4. Organising school improvement conferences, supplying mid-day meals, uniforms, free textbooks and writing materials to needy girl children.
5. The Central and State Governments should join hands and seek the cooperation of different voluntary organisations for the expansion of girls education in every nook and corner of the country.
6. The media can play a great role both in creating awareness about women's problems and fighting injustice against them.
7. Progressive laws should be passed to fight against women, insult, or harassment of women and other unhealthy of social customs and traditions.

REFERENCES

1. Das, K.K., *Current Problems in Indian Education*, Scientific Book Depot, Cuttack, Year 1984.
2. Nanda, S.K., *Indian Education and Its Problems Today*, Kalyani Publishers, New Delhi, Year 1977.
3. Das, C.R. & Mishra, Manoj, "*Forest Resources: Economic Benefits and Deprivation of Tribal Women:" Some Issue*, Year 2002.
4. Government of India, Ministry of Finance, Economic Division, 2002, Economic Survey, Year 2003-2004 and 2004-2005.
5. Government of Orissa (2001), Report on Time Use Survey, Directorate of Economics and Statistics.

6. Lekhi, R.K. *The Economics of Development and Planning,* Kalyani Publishers, New Delhi, Year 2005.

7. Dutta, Rudra & Sundaram, K.P.M., Indian Economy. S. Chand and Sons, New Delhi, Year 2002.

8. Annual Action Plan, PMRY, DIC, Ganjam, Year 2003-04 and 2004-05.

2

Education for Indian Women

A Study on Technology Education

Dr. S.N. Pathi*

Dr. A.K. Sahu**

Introduction

It is no doubt that women are performing a key role in growth and progress of a nation. They not only carry the generation but also contribute a lot in making the generation progressive and effective. A nation cannot progress without giving proper emphasis on their health and education. Good health provides a healthy generation and good education establishes a civilized society. Thus at this juncture when India projects herself as a fastest growing developing nation in the Asian continent it is our duty to make an in-depth study on the status of women and their educational status in our country with special reference to IT education as today's age is the age of technology and IT education occupies a special choice for all career conscious students.

Objectives of the Study

The objective of the present study to highlight the women education in India with a special reference to IT education. In the beginning, a review has been made from different literatures,

* Reader in Department of Business Administration Berhampur University.

** Reader in Department of Business Administration Berhampur University.

journals, books regarding the status of women in India. Thrust has been made to highlight how women education is the key success in growth and progress of a nation. Finally information has been provided regarding the inclination of women towards IT education, as it is the education of today's age.

Status of Women in India

It has been a mere four decades since the first rebellious voices were raised in protest against a male dominated society. The movement is raised for the last forty years for women freedoms. Of course it is not to say that there were not any voices raised prior to the movement for the women liberation. It is Rabindranath Tagore, one of our greatest poets, expressed the pains and inequality of the situation more than three quarters of a century ago when he wrote:

"O Lord, Why have you not given women the right to conquer her destiny?

Why does she have to wait head bowed?

By the roadside, Waiting with tired patience.

Hopping for a miracle in the morrow?"

However, if one looks at the history of the struggle for women's rights both in India and the world, it is this short span of the last four decades that has been the most eventful in terms of both bringing about the necessary shifts in thinking and in the achievement of practical policy changes with specific reference to women. From the fervent Feminism of the sixties to the introspection on the status of women in the seventies, to women-in-development debates in the eighties and to focuses on gender issues in the nineties, Forty years may have been a short but nonetheless momentous transition. An ancient Sanskrit saying says, woman is the home and the home is the basis of society. It is as we build our homes that we can build our country. If the home is inadequate-either inadequate in material goods and necessities or inadequate in the sort of friendly, loving atmosphere that every child needs to grow and develop, then that country cannot have harmony and no country which does not have harmony can grow in any direction at all. That is why women's education is almost more important than the education of boys and men. Our beloved Prime Minister Jawaharlal Nehru once said, "You can tell the condition of a nation by looking at the status of its women." However much a mother may love her children, it is all but impossible for her to provide high-quality child care if she herself is poor and oppressed, illiterate and uniformed, anemic and unhealthy, has five or six other children, lives in a slum or shanty, has neither clean water nor safe sanitation, and if she is without the necessary support either from health services, or from her society, or from the father of her children. The main reason for this is: Women are uneducated and they receive far less education than men, due both to social norms and fears of violence. Parents' reluctance to educate daughters has its roots in the situation of women. Parents have several incentives for not educating their daughters. Foremost is the view that education of girls brings no returns to parents and that their future roles, being mainly reproductive and perhaps including agricultural labour, require no formal education. As more and more boys are engaged in education, there is a growing reliance on the labour of girls. Girls are increasingly replacing their brothers on the farm while carrying on their usual responsibilities in housework. A large proportion of the roughly 40 million "nonworking" girls who are not in school are kept at home because of responsibilities in housework. Another disincentive for sending daughters to school is a concern for the protection of their virginity. When schools are located at a distance, when teachers are male, and when girls are expected to study along with boys, parents are often unwilling to expose their daughters to the potential assault on their virginity. As UN Secretary General Kofi Annan has stated, "Gender equality is more than a goal in itself. It is a precondition for meeting the challenge of reducing poverty, promoting sustainable development and building good governance." There are several clear indicators of the fact that Indian women continue to be discriminated against: the sex ratio is skewed against them; maternal mortality is the second highest in the world; more than 40 per cent of women are illiterate; and crimes against women are on the rise. Yet, the women's movement, which gathered strength after the 1970s, has led to progressive legislation and positive change, spurred on by the participation of women in local-self government. It is a paradox of modern India that women wield power and hold positions at the topmost levels, yet large sections of women are among the most underprivileged. Some women from the upper classes had political parties and command large followings, yet women's representation in the Parliament and state legislatures has not been more than 10 per cent. The roots of discrimination against women lie in the religious and cultural practices of India. The beginning of changes started with the reform movements in the nineteenth century, which addressed practices like *sati*, child marriage, life of the widows, etc. The status of women in the contemporary on text is reflected in the state of their health, education, employment and life in society.

The Indian women's movement started with addressing the problems that women faced, like violence, property rights, legal status, political participation, and the rights of minority women. Today, Indian women have won several victories against an oppressive way of life and are poised to raise pertinent questions that will make their lives more emancipating. The clearest indicator of discrimination against Indian women is the skewed sex ratio. There were only 927 females per 1000 males in India (the world average is 990 women per 1000 men), according to the 1991 Census Provisional figures for Census 2001 indicate that the trend has been slightly arrested, with the sex ratio at 933 females per 1000 males, with Kerala at 1058 females. This is welcome news. Yet cause for concern remains. The sex ratio of the 0 to 6 age group has declined sharply from 945 in 1991 to 927 in 2001. One reason for the adverse juvenile sex ratio is the increasing reluctance to have female children. Portable ultrasound machines and sex determination tests have made possible to detect and abort the female foetus. Social neglect of women and girls is the other contributing factor.

Women Education in India

In 1951, shortly after independence, the Census recorded that only 25 per cent of men and 7 per cent of women were literate. By the 1991 Census, female literacy had risen to 39 per cent. Census 2001 provisional figures indicate that 54.16 per cent of women are now able to read and write. Still, 245 million Indian women cannot read or write, comprising the world's largest number of unlettered women. National averages in literacy conceal wide disparities. For instance, while 95 per cent of women in Mizoram are literate, only 34 per cent of women in Bihar can read and write. Since the majority of India's unlettered people are female, literacy and education programmes need to focus on girls and women. Yet progressive government programmes like the Mahila Samakhya that designed a scheme to concise and empower rural women and motivate them to educate themselves, have been distorted in recent years. The District Primary Education Programme focuses on enrolment but not on the retention of girls in schools. In the absence of an enabling and empowering environment, girls are unlikely to stay on in school. The average Indian female has only 1.2 years of schooling, while the Indian male spends 3.5 years in school. More than 50 per cent girls drop out by the time they are in middle school. Women's organisations point out that sibling care is a major reason for girls dropping out of school and suggest that creches be attached to schools so that girls are free to attend classes. Midday meals, free books and uniforms, and the provision of toilets are other facilities suggested to bring more girls into the school system, besides more same sex schools and more female teachers. The women's movement has repeatedly called upon the government to fulfil its pledge to invest 6 per cent of the country's GDP in education. But in fact expenditure on education fell from 3.4 per cent of GDP in 1989-90 to 2.8 per cent in 1995-96. Further, amounts actually made available and real spending falls far short of budgetary provision.

In India women and girls receive far less education than men, due both to social norms and fears of violence. The country has the largest population of non-school-going working girls. India's constitution guarantees free primary school education for both boys and girls up to age 14. This goal has been repeatedly reconfirmed, but primary education in India is not universal. Overall, the literacy rate for women is 54.16 per cent versus 65.38 per cent for men, according to the census report 2001. There are several clear indicators of the fact that Indian women continue to be discriminated against; the sex ratio is skewed against them; maternal mortality is the second-highest in the world; more than 40 per cent of women are illiterate; and crimes against women are on the rise. Yet, the women's movement, which gathered strength after the 1970s has led to progressive legislation and positive change, spurred on by the participation of women in local self-government Eradication of female illiteracy has been one of the major concerns of the government of India since independence. The government and non-governmental organisations have established a number of initiatives for the educational development of women and girls. India is rich in policies, thus almost every conceivable strategy to promote girls' education has been covered. The problem lies in implementation. It is therefore necessary to concentrate on making the system work and deliver the services.

National Policy for the Empowerment of Women

Goals and Objectives

The goal of this Policy is to bring about the advancement, development and empowerment of women. The policy will be widely disseminated so as to encourage active participation of all stakeholders for achieving its goals. Specifically, the objectives of this policy include: Equal access to women to health care, quality education at all levels, career and vocational guidance, employment, equal remuneration, occupational health and safety, social security and public office etc.

A. Economic Empowerment of Women in

(i) *Agriculture*

(ii) *Support services* like child care facilities, including crèches at work places and educational institutions, homes for the aged and the disabled will be expanded and improved to create an enabling environment and to ensure their full cooperation in social, political and economic life.

(iii) *Science and technology* programmes to be organised to bring about a greater involvement of women in science and technology. These will include measures to motivate girls to take up science and technology for higher education and also ensure that development projects with scientific and technical inputs involve women fully. Efforts to develop a scientific temper and awareness should also be stepped up. Special measures should be taken for their training in areas where they have special skills like communication and information technology. Efforts to develop appropriate technologies suited to women's needs as well as to reduce their drudgery must be given a special focus too.

Social Empowerment of Women

Education

Equal access to education for women and girls must be ensured. Special measures must be taken to eliminate discrimination, universalise education, eradicate illiteracy, create a gender-sensitive educational system, increase enrollment and retention rates of girls and improve the quality of education to facilitate life-long learning as well as development of occupation/vocation/technical skills by women. Reducing the gender gap in secondary and higher education should be a focus area.

Institutional Mechanisms

Institutional mechanisms, to promote the advancement of women, which exist at the Central and State levels, must be strengthened. These will be through interventions as may be appropriate and will relate to, among others, provision of adequate resources, training and advocacy skills to effectively influence macro-policies, legislation programmes etc. to achieve the empowerment of women.

Thrust on Employment and Training for Women

In line with the Eighth Plan strategy, the nodal Department of Women and Child Development has reset its priorities to accord special emphasis on employment and income generation activities for women. The ultimate objective in all these efforts is to make women economically independent and self-reliant.

Support to Training and Employment Projects (STEP)

The programme of STEP, launched in 1987, aims to upgrade the skills of poor women, mobilise, concretise and provide employment on a sustainable basis to women in traditional sectors such as– agriculture, dairying, fisheries, sericulture, handlooms and handicrafts. In addition to training and empowerment support, the three special features which this programme includes are– 'gender sensitisation, 'women in development (WID) inputs' and provision of 'support services'.

Training-cum-Employment-cum-Production Centres (NORAD)

The second major programme of Training-cum-Employment-cum-Production Centres', which is commonly known as 'NORAD' assisted Training Programmes for Women' extends financial assistance to public sector undertakings/corporations/ autonomous bodies/voluntary organisations to train women in non-traditional trades and provide employment on a sustainable basis. Priority is given on training in areas like electronics, electrical, watch assembly and manufacturing, computer programming, printing and binding, handlooms, garment making, weaving and spinning, hotel management, fashion technology and tourism. Since the inception of the programme in 1983, more than 50,000 women and girls have benefited from training as well as employment opportunities provided under this scheme.

Socio-Economic Programme

The third major programme of employment and training for women is the Socio-Economic Programme (SEP) implemented by the Central Social Welfare Board (CSWB). SEP provides 'work and wage' to needy women such as destitute, widows, economically backward and the handicapped. Since the inception of the programme, 154,000 literate and illiterate women have been given 'wage and work' in the traditional as well as agro-based and non-traditional industries.

Condensed Courses of Education and Vocational Training for Adult Women (CCE & VT)

The scheme of condensed courses of education and vocational training for adult women started in 1958 and was recast and redefined by the CSWB in 1975. This scheme aims to provide new vistas of employment through continuing education and vocational training for women and girls who are school dropouts. Since the inception of this programme, about 80,000 adult women and young girls have undergone vocational training.

Women and Information Technology in India

India is well known for its vibrant information technology industry. Women's ability to participate in the country's IT growth is determined by the low status ascribed to women and girls in Indian society and the extreme poverty and poor IT infrastructure that restrict women's areas to education and information technology. Continued investment in IT infrastructure, greater availability of IT training, and creation of jobs will help the benefits of IT to women in India.

Current Indicators

- 34 per cent female adult literacy
- 38 per cent female secondary school enrolment
- 44 per cent youth literacy
- 36 per cent of tertiary students are female
- 30.4 per cent tertiary students in natural sciences are female
- 19 per cent female teaching staff at tertiary
- 23 per cent of India's internet users are women

Source: India's Internet: Ready for Explosive Growth, ISP planet, www.isp-planet.com

Affording girls and women access to basic education and literacy in India is the foremost obstacle to women's access to IT job opportunities. Education and literacy are low for both men and women, with women's literacy rate at only 51.4 per cent compared to men's 74.5 per cent. While enrolment rates have increased at the primary level for boys and girls, upper primary enrolment drops off, particularly for girls. Moreover, only 48 per cent of girls stay in the system until the secondary level. These statistics also vary widely between specific states within the country, where particularly the Northern and Eastern states have the lowest health and education indicators.

As most Indian women lack literacy and basic education, more advanced or specialised IT education is out of the reach of poorer women and only realistic for those middle class women and elite who can afford it in some form. Currently IT education and training is available in degree programmes in engineering colleges and universities and in diploma and certificate courses at polytechnics, and commercial and government training centres. Due to cost and selectivity of admissions at universities and engineering colleges, most Indian women are able to access IT training through training centres or women's polytechnics. However, not surprisingly, the quality of the training varies with each option. As the job market has become more competitive, certificates from training centres, or even diplomas in IT subjects from polytechnics, often do not equip job seekers with the competitive skills to guarantee a job, not to mention a well paid job. Moreover, the majority of women pursue their studies in the humanities and business rather than IT-related fields. Women make 88 per cent of the students in the arts, science and commerce, while education and law account for 4 per cent of women students, and engineering accounts only for 1 per cent.

The central government plans to upgrade the higher education institutions providing IT education and training will establish more IITs throughout the country and improve the regional engineering colleges. These efforts should strengthen the caliber of IT training available to Indian elites, but will have little impact on the majority of women, for who increased access to computers and secondary school education is needed. Insufficient phone lines and lack of other telecommunications infrastructure make Internet access a major challenges for both men and women in India. Most Indians live in rural areas, where infrastructure is poorer, and lack time and mobility to travel to public Internet facilities. India's one billion people only own 4.3 million computers and has access to only 26 million fixed phone lines. According to the Ministry of Information Technology, there are only 24 telephones for every 1,000 people in India, far fewer than the world average of 150 phones. Of those Indians who could access the Internet in India in the year 2000, only 23 per cent were women. Women in India make up 31 per cent of the official workforce. According to December 2000 estimates by Hindu Business Line.com, women comprised 19 per cent of the information technology work force in India, primarily within the software sector. Their overall median age in 25.7 years. According to Nasscom predictions, the male-female ratio in information technology jobs will be 65 men to 35 women by the year 2005. Women already comprise 37 per cent of the employees in IT-enabled service sector. Seeking to address the significant obstacles girls and women face in Indian society, the Government of India has programmes and policies that strive to improve women's status. The Ministry of Education has informal and formal education programmes for women and girls working in collaboration with non-government institutions. The Department of Women and Child Development is devoted to "formulating plans, policies and programmes, enacting/amending legislation, guiding and coordinating the efforts of both governmental and non-governmental organisations working in the field of Women and Child Development." The department also implements programmes in the areas of welfare and support services, training for employment and income generation, awareness generation and gender sensitisation. The state of Andhra Pradesh has reserved 33 per cent of places in all higher education institutions for women: a noteworthy policy that may encourage women to enroll in advanced IT education programmes which they would normally be unlikely to pursue. Other data on specific IT and women government programmes were not available. As the largest democracy in the world, India has a huge array of non-government organisations active in education and women's issues. There have been numerous experiments in India devoted to addressing the digital divide, particularly because of the high-profile domestic IT industry juxtaposed to the extremely poor and uneducated population. However, only a few are starting to specifically target women.

Conclusion

There is no second thought that the women education is very important for societal growth. When the women are empowered, society with stability will get assured. The Government must ensure the continuity of secondary education and university education for girls. It is essential to establish connectively between the university and secondary schools. Distance education packages have to be evolved to cater towards women education for reaching remote areas. Periodically, secondary level students should be counselled to continue their education both in diploma and degree level. In our country, women constitute 48 per cent of the total population. Now-a-days women are entering in every field. They are becoming doctors, engineers, advocates, teachers; political leaders, administrators, police officials, professionals and they also have joined the Armed Forces. Enlightened women are very important for nation building since their thoughts, the way of working and value system will lead to faster development of a good family, good society and a good nation. Thus, the women in our country have tremendous opportunity for participating in the development of the nation. Information technology education makes them more enthusiastic and most of the girl students are offering for the said course. Government is also trying to explore more avenues for them. Most of the State Government have made reservations for them so that they can move at par with boys. Now-a-days banks are also financing for their education so that parents will not hesitate for their education. However, the scope has not reached to rural women. Even primary education is a dream for most of the rural girls. Little care has been given for their health and education. This leads to social disparity. Government must take active steps for removing any stumbling blocks in this regard. We all know education to a boy is limited to him only, where as a girl can educate a family. The present twenty-first century will be a more advanced period in Indian society. India is going to be a super power in every angle. Even the developed nations of the world are admitting India's potential. Women, instead of sitting at their homes, should come forward and fight for their legitimate rights of getting all types of education starting from primary to higher education of their choice. In this way they are not only educating themselves but also educating the whole nation. Thus as a responsible citizen of this motherland, it is our duty to cooperate at every sphere to attain the desired goal and we have to see that all rural, semi-urban and urban girls have got proper education. Further scope of education in different fields is to be opened for them. Then only we can dream a *Mahan Bharat*.

REFERENCES

1. Chitnis, Suma, ed.; Altbach G., ed.

   Higher Education Reform in India: Experience and Perspective, New Delhi, Sage Publications, 1993. 438 p.

2. *Development of Women Education in India,* Premchand Patanjali. N.D. Shree Publisher, 2005, Vol. II, 280.
3. *Empowerment of Women in India*—A Speech by Dr. Abraham George Addressed at New Mexico U.S.A. on 2001.
4. *Growth of Higher Education in India* PIB Press Release.htm.
5. *India Case Study*.htm.
6. *India Social Objective*.htm.
7. *National Initiatives Concerning the Equality of Opportunities in Education/ Training in India*—Department of Women and Child Development and ILO.
8. *The National Policy of Education*—1986, Programme of Action.
9. Agrawal, S.P.; Aggarwal, J.C. *Development of Education in India, Vol. 4: Select Documents,* 1993-94, New Delhi, Concept Publishing Company, 1997, 447 p.
10. Aggarwal, J.C., *Education in Emerging India,* New Delhi, Doaba House, 1994, 222 p.
11. *Chronic Hunger and the Status of Women in India,* Carol S. Coonrod, June 1998.
12. Times of India. *"Protest Against Atrocities in Women."* Internet. p. 3.
13. Desai, Sonalde. 1994. *Gender Inequalities and Demographic Behaviour: India.* New York: The Population Council, Inc.
14. Evolution of Enlightened Women-*Speech of Honorable President of India Dr. A.P.J. Abdul Kalam Addressed at the Golden Jubilee Function of RBVRR Women's College on 5-8-2005 at Hyderabad.*

3

Marital Rape

The Legal Domestic Violence

Prof. R.P. Sharma

Women form about fifty per cent of the society. Without their literacy, empowerment and security economic development cannot be accelerated. Even though social system has been improving over the centuries exploitation of women at home and outside has not been reduced considerably. Rape is one of the cruel atrocities on women. This phenomenon is not of the present day world, it has been there in the society from the ancient days. Rape is an animal behaviour. Man has formed his own society, became civilized and has adopted strict social laws but so far not able to control the wild temptation for rape. With the increase in the social development the cases of rape and other atrocities on women is on increase.

The number of crimes in Orissa has not shown any decline in spite of expansion of police network. The over all number of crimes in Orissa has been fluctuating from year to year but on an average the crimes remained 52,909 annually from 1993 to 2003 and declined by about 2.85 per cent. (Table—3.1) The atrocities on women form about 6.24 per cent of the total crimes. (Table—3.2) The rapes form about 37.94 per cent of atrocities on women in the year 2003. It is a fact that all rape cases are not reported to the police due to social taboo. Marital rape is a new dimension of rape which is not generally coming to the light but it is a torture on women and violation of human right of women which has not been given importance under torture of women.

Table 3.1 Growth of Crimes in Orissa, 1993-2003

Year	*No. of crimes*	*Growth*	*Per cent*
1993	53,872	–	–
1994	51,161	-2711	-5.14
1995	53,614	2453	16.17
1996	53,196	-418	-0.77
1997	54,049	853	1.60
1998	53,679	-370	-0.68
1999	52,672	-1007	-1.87
2000	54,157	1485	2.81
2001	51,357	-2800	-5.17
2002	51,912	-555	-1.08
2003	52,337	425	0.81

Source: Statistical Outline of Orissa, 2003, Govt. of Orissa, Bhubaneswar.

Table 3.2: Atrocities on Women in Orissa

Year	*Rape*	*Dowry*	*Non-dowry*	*Other*	*Total*	*Per cent to all crimes*
1999	1321	900	498	440	3159	6.00
2000	1219	875	445	410	2949	5.44
2001	1306	889	452	489	3136	6.10
2002	1219	1030	552	468	3269	6.29
2003	1239	1042	524	461	3266	6.24

Source: Statistical Outline of Orissa, 2003, Govt. of Orissa, Bhubaneswar.

Marital Rape

Many a wife, in a domestic set up face atrocities from the husband in the form of forcible sexual intercourse or what it is termed as Marital Rape. Statistics are not available on the marital rape as it is a delicate domestic affair, but it is a fact and it exists in the society, perhaps from the inception of marriage as an institution in the human society. Even though it is invisible, in the sense that the cases are not reported in the press or cases are filed with the police, the marital rape exists both in the lower class families as well as in the higher levels of the society.

When the marital rape become unbearable, as a last resort the women especially in the urban families are compelled to file divorce suits. In these cases some facts are revealed with regard to marital rape. The main complaints are:

1. The husbands demand unlimited sexual intercourse and demand in such situation also when the wife is ailing, observing some religious festivals. The husband demands sex with intake of high alcoholic drinks and sexual intercourse is done cruelly; instead of pleasure it becomes a cruel torture for the wife.
2. The husband refuses to use contraceptives even when the wife insists. Never adopts other family control devises which force the wife to conceive and bear more children making the economic condition of the family miserable.
3. Wives also complain that the husbands force upon them to resort to unnatural sex, against their will which is wild, cruel and painful.

There is no law in the country to recognise forcible sexual intercourse by a husband with his wife as offence. The traditional common law defines rape: *"A man engaged in sexual intercourse with a women, 'other than his wife' by force or threat of force against the will of the woman and without her consent."* Same forcible sexual intercourse on his wife is not regarded as rape legally. The law does not recognise the right of the wife to refuse forcible sexual act by the husband.

The Constitution of India has the following two articles which guarantees the fundamental rights to every citizen but in case of marital rape these rights are violated for the women as wife.

1. *Article 14:* Equality before law irrespective of caste, creed, religion, economic status or sex.
2. *Article 19:* Right to freedom.

In legal punishment system of India marital rape is not regarded as offence and hence there is no punishment for the domestic rapists: whatever legal provisions are there presently are not anyway helpful to the adult wife. The provisions are:

(a) In the 19th century when the child marriage was the norm in the society. The Child Marriage Act forbidden the husband to have forcible sexual intercourse with the wife if the latter's age is less than 10 years. There were cases where the bride died because of forcible sexual intercourse but the husband escaped punishment because the wife was above 10 years of age according to legal provision.

(b) In the Indian Penal Code, Article 375 increased the age limit of the wife to 15 years. This means if a husband has forcible sexual intercourse with his wife whose age is more than 15 years of age, it is not regarded as rape.

Can it be Prevented?

For women, especially in the Hindu social system the husband has special place:

1. Husband is worshipped like God.
2. Pleasing the husband is regarded as the sacred duty of the wife and denying sexual or other whims regarded as sin.
3. When the husband is the main income earner to the family a wife cannot go against the whims/forcible sexual intercourse for fear of economic insecurity.

In these circumstances any legal provision to prevent marital rape will not be successful. No wife will come forward to lodge a complaint against her husband on marital rape, except of course at the last resort in case of divorce. The social and women's organisations pressing for a legal provision forbidding marital rape. It is difficult to detect marital rape as there would not be any complaint from the wife formally. A third party, other than wife, that is wife's parents and women's organisations, can lodge a complaint but it is very difficult to prove it unless the wife comes forward to confess it, which she will not do. Even though legal provisions forbidding martial rape cannot be enforced, the women's organisations believe that a legal provision will influence the husband's behaviour to some extent and restrain him from cruel sexual action. In the tribal communities the Headman of the village meeting sanctions punishments on the torturing of wife and children, and also in case of marital rape when it is injurious to wife. Of course still the remote tribal communities are free societies and the wife can leave the husband simply informing the Headman of the community and go for another husband, which is not possible for a wife in the civil society.

Presently the Government of India contemplating to make some legal protection to the wife and punishment for the husband for domestic sexual violence. After the Bharatiya Janata Party's suggestion for the provision of death penalty for the rapist, nation-wide debate is going on to include marital rape as a criminal offence and certain checks for its prevention. The proposed Bill to be introduced in the Parliament, Violence Against Women (Prevention) Bill which includes domestic violence. The women's organisations are demanding to include "sexual intercourse against the will of the wife" as one of the domestic violences. The National Commission for Women has also send a draft bill to the Government of India to include marital rape under domestic violence and to provide some protection measures to the wife.

Legal provision is not just enough. Even though more than century ago the child marriages are banned legally and today a higher marriageable age has been fixed legally; child marriages are going on and under age marriages could not be prevented. Provision of legal restrictions cannot prevent marital rape, just fear of punishment, unless the wife acquires the economic independence and conscious about it.

The National Commission for Women has taken some initiatives in this regard to educate the young girls, unmarried ones, to acquaint them regarding happiness and hazards in marriage. A short-term course is designed, not just sex education, about all aspects of family life after marriage to the conducted in the colleges of Delhi for the students. But what about millions of women folk, not educated, no economic status and had to depend on the earnings of husband, in the rural India, and also in the urban slums? How to help them? Can they come forward to protect their rights, if at all they realise that it is their fundamental right?

4

Women Education and Development

Mrs. Babilata Shroff*

Female Education and Development—A Case Study of Titilagarh

Education is not a product; marks, degree/diploma, job: money—in that order it is a process, a never-ending one. The process begins right from conception up to the last breath for learning never ends. Real education helps us to develop our sensitivity to the problems outside. It creates conditions for the development of a wholesome personality so that a man/woman can contribute his/her best to the family, society and the nation.

Men and women are the two wheels of the society. If one of the two falls defective the society cannot progress. Hence we need education for the females as we need for the males. "Teach a man and you have taught only one, but teach a woman and you have taught a family;" goes a famous saying.

Most of the Indian women living in an orthodox and conservative family feel inhibited to raise their voice against aggressive dominance of the male persons of the society owing to their inferiority complex (being less educated and economically weaker than their male counterparts) and rigid code of conduct imposed upon them. Pens of many writers like Fakeer Mohan Senapati, Anita Desai, Arundhati Roy, Iqbal Unnisa Hussain, Jame Austen, Virginia Wolf and many others reflect this conservative attitude towards female education and travails of the subdued

* Lecturer in Economics, D.A.V. Colleges, Titilagarh.

women in a male dominated society. Some exposes and voices the need for emancipation and education for Indian women.

During the Vedic Era (Before 200 B.C.)

During the Vedic Era both boys and girls had equal opportunities for advanced education. The girls used to spend early years of their life in Brahmacharya Ashram after Upanayan Samskar Ceremony and were permitted to quit earlier as they were expected to marry at the age of 16 or 17. Women dominated teaching some were so learned that they publicly challenged men of letters in discussions on philosophical and metaphysical subjects. 27 women Rishis like Vishvarav Ghosh, Apala Atreyi, Indrani, Surya Savitri, composed the mantras for Vedas, especially the Rig Veda.

Education had provided women a higher status in the society. At that time India was considered a golden bird.

During Post-Vedic Period (200 B.C.—1200 A.D.)

The ancient Indian lawgiver Manu equated the household duties with Yajna. As the girls marry at an early age they would not be able to learn the mantras properly, and would make mistakes. From that education for girls, lost importance. Gradually the age at marriage dropped down to 12. Except the female folk from the rich and noble families all others were deprived of good education.

Medieval Period (1200-1800 A.D.)

The tragedy travail started during this period with the introduction of "Purdah" by the orthodox male dominated Mughals. Female education was restricted only to some royal ladies. Razia Sultana, Gulbadan Begum, Noor Jehan, Mumtaz Mahal, Jahanara Begum and some others had really made some mark.

After 1800 A.D.

During the early 1800 A.D. the conditions of Indian women was very pitiable. Both women and the so-called untouchable were compared to drums and declared to be unfit for learning. Importance of women education fell down. Status of women went on declining. Abuses like child marriage, Sati, restrictions on widow remarriage went on increasing.

Good day came with the Social Reform movement under the active leadership of Raja Ram Mohan Roy and Ishwar Chandra Vidyasagar. They also did a lot for the expansion of female education. In 1802 David Hare started first school for girls in Calcutta. Improvements in this regard were made after the establishment of Indian Education Commission in 1882-1883. Still more progress was found when education came into Indian control in 1921.

Role of Christian Missionaries

Before the establishment of British Rule in India the Christian Missionaries were quite active. To satisfy their motives they made women their prime focus by opening Zenanas, i.e. women quarters.

Gandhiji's Attitude

During 1910-20 female education got fresh support from Gandhiji. His open acknowledgement that his concepts of passive resistance and non-violence were inspired by the lives of women (Stree Shakti). He called upon women to step out of the secure walls of their homes and join the freedom movement. The roles played by Kasturba, Aruna Asraf Ali, Baby Indira and many others were quite impressive. But majority of rural ladies unaffected.

Further Emancipation

During the post-war period, prejudices against women education and participation in the work force were weakened, when women's earnings came to be seen as a contribution, enabling the family to make ends meet. But the rural sector remained unaffected.

Gender equality is enshrined in our constitution and there are a plethora of legislations both at the central and state levels. It also made special provisions for protection of their lives, rights and empowerment.

In the Five Year Plans the Govt. of India consistently emphasised female education as one of the principal instruments to step up the status of women (which affect a lot to the development of the economy).

A country's Human Development Index and level of development are directly related to female education and female participation in the work force. Realising this a Women and Child Development Department is set up at the centre which implements a number of welfare programmes like Indira Mahila Yojana, Support to Training and Employment Programme for Women, Rastriya Mahila Kosh (encourages SHGs), Education Work for Prevention of Atrocities Against Women. Eradication of Commercial Sexual Exploitation of Women and Children, Prevention of Sexual Harassment at Work Place, etc.

UN and Women Education

The UN charter is the first international agreement which recognised gender equality as a fundamental human right.

Role of IWD

As a result of Industrial Revolution, female literacy as well as female participation in the work force increased. Development of trade unions for women during early 20th century and formation of organisations changed the scenario.

Gradually IWD was declared and celebrated each year on March 8. On 50th anniversary of IWD in 1960, a general and social rights of women was adopted IWD symbolises the strength of the women-kind and how they could be made equal partners for progress of the whole humanity.

Women Education: An Essential Ingredient of Development

Women education play an important role in the formation of future citizens. Women in the role of a mother assumes the dignity and decorum equivalent to that of Almighty. Once Napolean Bonaparte said, " Give me good mothers and I will give you a good nation." An educated mother would be able to teach, train and guide a child in a much better manner than an illiterate one. They would educate, train and polish for a tough life and develop their children for perfection.

The child learns his first lesson in the womb when the mother thinks, reads and does good, and grows sound when she works, exercises, eats, thinks, talks, sleeps and so on in a desirable manner. Here education helps a lot.

Then the child learns at the feet of his mother. He understands the world in his mother. He is a clean slate and anything can be written on it. Here an educated and prudent mother can only develop his life and career from jeopardy. History can not forget Jijabai's role in forming the great Maratha Warrior Shivaji.

It is found that with the passage of time human needs are increasing. It reminds every now and then to earn more or deprive the family of numerous needs and comforts. Here educated women extend a helping hand in sharing the household burdens and in increasing the standard of living. She also helps in preparing the family budget in a more economical manner.

Female participation in the work force makes them assets. Once who was considered a liability that must accompany some dowry is now considered a fruit-packed tree.

Female education also makes the housewives more responsible towards saving and investment in a much profitable manner.

Female literacy at ages 15 and over is quite positively correlated with percentage of female workers in modern occupations, age at marriage, not of children, health and nutrition of the family, and contraceptive use. It is strongly and negatively correlated with infant mortality and fertility. The Operation Research Group finds that birth rate in general are lower and adoption of family planning norms are more popular in those states where education is more wide spread. (e.g. Kerala).

Further lack of education among a majority of rural folk is mainly responsible for the population growth in India. Female literacy removes irrational ideas and religious superstitions. It widens the outlook towards cartelism and looks inter caste marriage in a liberal manner.

Female Education and Development: A Case Study of Titilagarh

According to the 2001 census Titilagarh NAC is sharing 10 Sq. k.m. total population 30,251 population in 15 wards and 2945 holdings. In 2004 total female illiterates in 1266 which includes female SC illiterates 228, female ST illiterates is 379 and the remaining general. This NAC has sufficient number of primary schools. High Schools and 2 colleges one of which is exclusively for girls.

Besides the NAC is carrying continuous Education Programme to bring more women into the category of literates. Eight Centres and one nodal centre are present which concentrate on education to illiterate women. 17 teachers are engaged in teaching. Each centre is having a library which provides various types of Oriya books (mainly Ramayana, Mahabharata, etc.) to the ladies. Still then all the illiterate ladies belong to the slums.

The effect of women education on development in Titilagarh is studied taking 150 women chosen from 6 different groups—25 in each group.

Group A = 25 working ladies mostly teachers, lecturers, doctors and others (excluding the class IV employees and labourers)

Group B = 25 women who are at least graduates but house wives

Group C = 25 under graduate house wives

Group D = 25 under matriculate housewives

Group E = 25 housewives who have not crossed primary education

Group F = 25 college girl students

A study on each group regarding their attitude towards family size/no. of children, gender bias, health and nutrition consciousness, age at marriage, eco-contribution towards the family, dowry, casteism, use of family planning devices, environmental protection and attitude towards saving and investment are made. The findings give a broad idea on female education, spread effect and development.

1. *Female Education and Number of Children:* All the groups (except E) favoured small family having 1 or 2 children. The consequence of population explosion is realised more as we move from Group E to D, C, B and A.

This is clearly seen in Table—4.1.

Table 4.1: Distribution of the no. of children in each group

Group	*No. of Children*			
	1	*2*	*3*	*More*
A	4	19	1	1
B	2	20	3	0
C	1	19	4	1
D	0	15	7	3
E	0	9	10	6

All are realising the possibilities of attaining a higher standard of living and getting more comforts having less nos. of children and low standard of living having more children.

Preference towards one or two children is almost equal for Gr. A and B. This attitude is falling with the fall in the level of education. It is too much for Gr. E. All the ladies in Gr. E belong to slums. They all know the advantage from TV campaigns, etc. but not yet accepted. Again in Groups. A and B the ladies accepted that there is a clash with the conservative attitude of some of their in-laws/elders towards a male child, no. of children and adoption of family planning measures.

Average no. of children in each group is shown below:

Group A	=	1.90
Group B	=	2.04
Group C	=	2.20
Group D	=	2.54
Group E	=	2.90

When plotted in a graph we get the following trend.

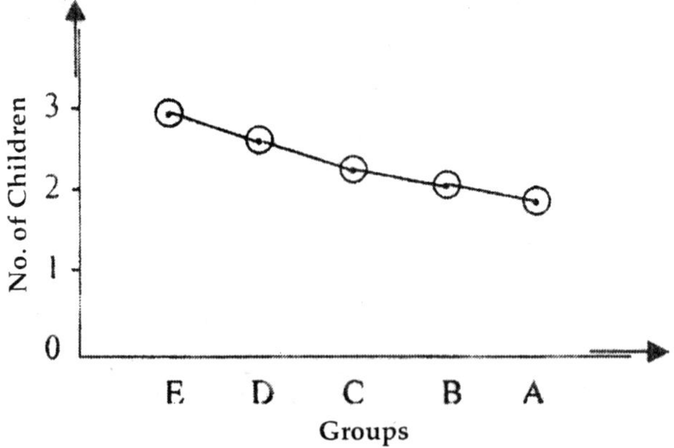

We find a negative correlation between female education and no. of children.

2. *Female Education and Gender Bias:* Group A and B are strongly indifferent towards the sex of the child. In these 2 groups i.e. in 50 cases 4 have 1 girl child each and 3 have 2 girl children each, 5 ladies admitted the bias towards a male child is under pressure. This bias increases as we move from Group C to D and E.

3. *Attitude towards Education and Female Education:* All the groups are in favour of education for both sexes but A, B, C and D groups are more sportive towards female education as compared for Gr. E ladies. The struggle for existence does not give pace to education for Gr. E children whether a male or a female child. The vicious circle of illiteracy, poverty, malnutrition and low standard of living continues. In spite of free education upto primary level, supply of free books upto class VII, Mid-day meal, etc., children in Gr. E are irregular in schools. Dropouts among them is more while demand for public school education is more for the Gr. A, B and C. Most of the child labourers are from Gr. E.

   Besides it is found that the children of Group A and B are doing better than other groups in curricular as well as extra curricular activities.

4. *Age at Marriage:* All the girls in Group F preferred marriage after completion of education (at least upto graduation level) and/or even after getting job. The average age at marriage for each group is:

Group A	=	25
Group B	=	23
Group C	=	20
Group D	=	18
Group E	=	16

When plotted in a graph

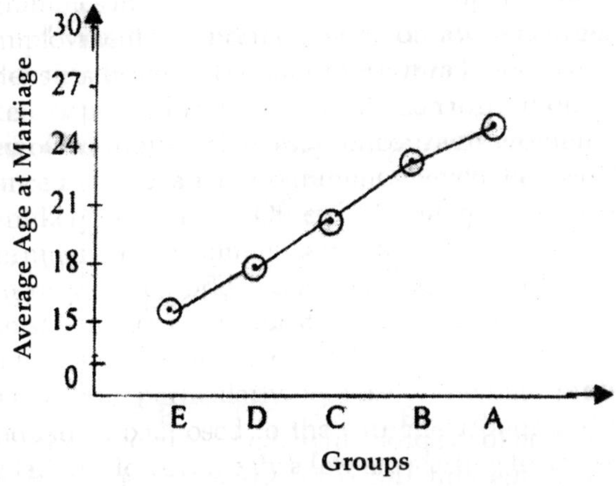

Hence there is a positive correlation between female education and age at marriage.

5. *Infant Mortality:* Average number of infants died in each group is given below:

Group A	=	0
Group B	=	0
Group C	=	0.4
Group D	=	0.6
Group E	=	1

Here we find a negative correlation between female education and infant mortality.

6. *Female Education and Attitude towards Health and Hygiene:* Except Gr. E almost all other ladies and cautious towards health i.e. safe drinking water, cleanliness etc. and hygiene. But the awareness goes on declining as we move from Gr. A and B towards E.

7. *Female Education and Economy Assets:* All the working ladies are sharing the family expenses and help in increasing their standard of living. They are providing more comfort which they would not provide to the family out of their husband's income only.

8. *Attitude towards Dowry:* Group A, B and F strongly protested dowry. Here education clashes with economic status. Most of the working ladies said that their marriages were dowryless and the Group F girls are also expecting a dowryless marriage.

9. *Environmental Awareness:* Group A, B and F are most conscious towards the degradation in the environment. They are also more conscious towards its protection than the other groups.

Conclusion

The solution to the problem of devt lies in our social texture. The Indian slums and the rural areas are the backlogs of underdevelopment in India. Women in these areas must be educated at least about health, nutrition, general hygiene and protection of environment. Besides knowledge on national and international events, importance of quality education, and information about developed women in other areas/nations may create a spread effect. Even in the present scenario women have made their influence felt in all walks of life, but retained the feminine graces—motherliness, wives' fidelity, kinship bonds, cultural norms and the ever cherished "home sweet home" instinct.

More stress should be given to help our girls in their glorious and difficult career of motherhood. Subjects like cookery, needlework, elementary knowledge of midwifery, child rearing etc. may be given at a higher stage except for girls of ability and interest in higher studies and research. Everywhere women should be encouraged to read newspapers. Nobody can deny the fact that female education is one of the most essential requirements of economic development.

REFERENCES

1. Psychological Exploration of Inner Mind of Indian Women: *A Feminist Perspective*; R.K. Mishra, Reader in English, DAV College, Titilagarh, Orissa.
2. India Today: Special Feature Jan' 05—*Emerging Women Power*.
3. India Today: April 4, 2005, *Power Goddess*.
4. CSR March '05–Current Issues and Topics of Social Relevance *"Education for Personality Development"*.
5. *Manu Samhita*.
6. Employment News, 5-12 March' 2005. –*"Frailty! Thy Name is not Woman"* by Amlanjyoti Majumdar, Dy. Director (Media) in the Ministry of Rural Development.
7. www.womenexceel.com
8. www.prod.kerala.gov.in
9. www.du.ac.in
10. www.bnca.ac.in
11. www.irana.ac.in
12. www.women-universitykar.nic.in
13. www.nite.in.org
14. www.bhu.ac.in
15. *Eco. Aspects of Dowry*: A Case Study. M.Phil. Dissertation Submitted to Berhampur University by Babilata Shroff.
16. *Psychological Foundations of Education*—B.D. Dash & B.M. Dash.
17. *Trends and Issues in Indian Education*—B.N. Das.
18. *Pivotal Issues in Indian Education*—S.K. Kochhar.
19. *History of Education in India*—B.N. Das, Dominant Publishers and Distributors, New Delhi–110 002.
20. *Education and Society*—B.N. Das, Dominant Publishers and Distributors, New Delhi–110 002.

5

Empowerment of Women
A Holistic Approach

Dr. Sandhya Rani Das

For centuries women in India are being suffering due to discrimination, exploitation and exposed to various kinds of harassment at various levels. Women constitute nearly half of the total population of the country and therefore the development of the country is not possible without the development of this vast segment. Today the development of women has been a major concern for our planners and policy makers. After independence our planners have envisaged various constitutional provisions to protect the interest of women and undertaken various socio-economic development measures for their upliftment. In addition, various voluntary organisations are also being working hard for emancipation of women. Despite all these efforts by the government as well as voluntary bodies, still majority of women are deprived of their minimum rights.

Women in India occupied an exalted status during the Vedic period and their status has been deteriorated gradually afterwards because of cultural and societal traits, ignorance, illiteracy and superstitions. The role of women in the socio-economic life of India and in other developing countries have for several decades been neglected by policy makers and the society at large. Even social scientists avoided issues concerning women *per se* and concentrated on women's activities that were considered worthy of research and women were described in terms of their relationship to those activities. However, in recent years there has been a growing recognition that women who form half of the society cannot be ignored. Things are moving on a right direction in India though slow in motion. This is a vision of a large number of intellectuals struggling to put together an agenda for future at philosophical, social, political, economic and religious planes.

The need of the hour is to change the mindset of the people which include both men and women towards improving the status of women. The term 'status' denotes relative position of persons in a social system or sub-system which is distinguishable from that of others through rights and obligations. In simple term "the position women enjoys in the society is her status". The major reason for the persistent low status of women may be attributed to:

- Gender biased societal norms
- Barriers encountered in accessing legal entitlements
- Persistent and institutionalised discrimination against the girl child
- Inadequacy of institutional mechanism for the advancement of women
- Poor participation by women in decision making structures and processes
- Gender biasness in macro-economic policies
- Feminisation of poverty
- Invisibility of women's contribution to the economy and environmental sustenance
- Gender gaps in literacy, education and health
- Growing trend of violence against women
- Negative portrayals and perpetuation of gender stereotypes of mass media

Various efforts are being made to enable women to play a greater role in development. Support services like nutrition, health, upgradation skills, income generating assets and opportunities for employment are being provided through various governmental programmes. These programmes seek to specially support those women who are heads of families and whose families living below the poverty line in rural areas. Rural development is one area where increased focus is placed on women because it is felt that unless their socio-economic status is raised, no tangible improvement can be brought about in the overall status of women in the country.

It is in this context, empowerment of women as a goal of women's development has been gaining wider acceptance. Empowerment means 'the process by which people take control and action to overcome obstacles. Empowerment especially refers to the collective action by the deprived and oppressed to overcome the obstacles of structural inequality which previously caused their disadvantaged position. It is a continuous and multi-dimensional process by which women able to realise their potential and overcome obstacles.

The parameters of empowerment are, developing the ability to think critically, building self-confidence, building up of group cohesion and fostering decision making and action; ensuring effective participation on social change; encouraging group action and providing infrastructure and climate for economic development. By empowerment women would be able to develop self-esteem confidence, realise their potential and enhance their collective bargaining power. Women's empowerment can be viewed of several interrelated and mutually reinforcing components. Succinctly the parameters of women empowerment are:

- Raising self-esteem and self-confidence of women.
- Elimination of discrimination and all forms of violence against women and girl child.
- Building and strengthening partnership with civil society particularly women's organisations.
- Enforcement of constitutional and legal provisions and safeguarding rights of women.
- Building a positive image of women in the society and recognising their contributions in social, economic and political sphere.
- Developing ability among women to think critically.

- Fostering decision making and collective action.
- Enabling women to make informed choices.
- Ensuring women's participation in all walks of life.
- Providing information, knowledge, skills for self-employment.
- Elimination of discrimination against women's participation in the areas of:
  - Access to food
  - Equal wages
  - Property rights
  - Family resources
  - Freedom of movement and travel
  - Access to credit
  - Control over savings, earnings and resources
  - Guardianship and custody of children and their maintenance
- Gender sensitisation training in schools, colleges and other professional institutions for bringing about institutional changes.

Women are to be empowered in more than one ways. Feminists talk of different kinds of empowerment: Integrated development, economic empowerment and conscious raising and organising. These approaches are not mutually exclusive. The approach of one kind depends on how it interprets the causes of women's powerlessness and what sort of interventions needed for their empowerment. Whatever may be the approach the final goal of almost all approaches is to raise the quality of life of women and to enable them to participate in the process of development and nation building. In short a holistic approach is needed which ensures their social, economic, political and cultural development.

Empowerment through Education

In the words of Herbert Spencer "Education" is a training for the completeness of life. It brings perfection to life which means the growth and development of personality. It qualifies a person to fulfil central economic, political and cultural functions and thereby improves the socio-economic status of the people. It also helps to equalise the status of individuals who belong to different social strata.

It needs no emphasis that education plays a very crucial role in the process of women's empowerment. However, literacy, among women presents a dismal picture. According to 2001 Census, male literacy has gone up to 75.85 per cent whereas for females it has reached only 54.16 per cent. This clearly shows gender disparity in educational development. Women of our country trapped in illiteracy and social deprivation, tend to loss awareness and motivation and this makes them weak, isolated, vulnerable and powerless. Therefore, there is a need to undertake special measures to improve enrolment/retention rates, as school dropouts continue to be high. For ensuring easy access to education among girl child, provision of hostels, crèches and other infrastructural facilities should receive priority. The girl child should be assisted through scholarships/financial assistance, free books and other such provisions.

Educational facilities provided to women should take into account their special needs. Employment oriented education and diversified vocational training should receive special emphasis. Job oriented condensed courses are most appropriate in this context. Rehabilitation programmes with vocational training for alternative jobs with sustainable income should be taken up.

While preparing women for better future, it is essential to give them what is known as life skill education. These are the skills that helps women to deal with the demands and challenges of everyday life. More specifically these include problem solving and decision making skills that would enable the girls to make judicious decisions in all areas of life. Critical thinking and creative thinking skills would help them to arrive at these decisions. Self-awareness, empathy, communication and interpersonal relationship skills, and skills for coping with stress will improve their productivity, efficiency, self-esteem and self-confidence. Today, school education consists of mostly imparting information which does not necessarily prepare them for living a healthy life. Therefore, a definite attempt has to be made to give children the skills for healthy and happy thinking.

Political Empowerment

It is an undenying fact that women played a very crucial role in our freedom struggle. When India got its independence several women leaders occupied prominent positions and the constitution given them equal rights and legitimised their roles for participation. Despite all these developments, women's representation in the formal political structure has remained marginal. In our parliament women's representation is very limited. Till recent elections their representation never crossed eight per cent. Only in the latest election that held in 1999 their number has become 47, but still not reached the 10 per cent mark. The conditions is more or less same regarding their representation to various state legislative assemblies.

The 73rd Amendment to the Constitution reserved a minimum one third representation for women in the membership as well as positions of Chairpersons of Panchayats at all the three levels namely the village, district and intermediate levels gives representation to women in a "critical mass". Reservation created a space for women's need within the structural framework of politics and his legitimised women's issued but women to be aware of their political power. Reservation for women in the electoral process is undoubtedly a positive step that needs to be extended to the state assemblies and parliament. However, a more comprehensive view is required including equal emphasis on economic rights of women. Otherwise the inherent potential of the policy of enhancing the participation of women will not be fully realised.

The Panchayati Raj Institutions are the prime movers of decentralisation at the grassroots level. The main aim of Panchayati Raj Institutions is to accelerate the pace of development and involve all segments of population in the process so that their needs and aspirations can be fulfilled. The participation of women in these bodies ensures efficient, equitable and sustainable community oriented development. Their involvement provides them opportunity, autonomy and freedom to decide for themselves.

However, the participation of women in the potential process has been severely limited.

Participation of women in the Panchayati Raj has immediate as well as long term implications. Women can be instrumental in upgrading the quality of village leadership by raising their voice against corruption and exploitation. However, in rural areas despite their inclination to participate in the political process, they could not able to do so because of their preoccupation in family and farm activities. In addition certain factors like caste, federalism, apathy and family status do come in the way. Though the Constitution of India provided them equal status, it is yet to be realised this equality and equal participation in the political process at the grassroot level.

It is in this context, political participation of women is necessary not only for their development and improving their status, but also for their mass participation in the national development. Political empowerment leads to realise their creative potential and make them economically independent. Therefore there is a need to create political consciousness among women and motivate them to actively participate in the democratic process. Entry into political process will constitute the first step for their empowerment. Once they are politically empowered they will realise themselves as full, equal citizens and play their role in changing the political structure in their favour.

Economic Empowerment

The low status of women in large segments of Indian society cannot be raised without opening up independent employment and income generating activities to cater their needs and aspirations. This fact has been realised by our planners and a plethora of economic development programmes for the emancipation of women has been initiated. However, these programmes lacked the gender sensitivity and failed to cater to the needs of women. They are designed and implemented without taking into account different needs of women identifying their different biological and sociological differences. It is in this context, the need of the hour is to design gender sensitive development interventions where policy makers planners and analysts must constantly check their preconceived notions. They must keep in mind the ground realities, while designing the women's development programmes. This is necessary in order to avoid the negative impact of their own preconceptions and prejudices.

Our past experience shows that most of the economic development programmes based on technocratic approach failed to give desired result due to neglect of human dimension in the process. Therefore, what is required is a humanistic approach which ensures the participation and involvement of women at every stage of development process—for planning to evaluation.

Economic empowerment has two aspects. One is income or livelihood. The other is whether or not women have effective control over this income or livelihood. The parameters of economic empowerment of women are:

- Provide information and knowledge on various self-employment and income generating activities.
- Provide information on support services.
- Educate and motivate women to undertake income generating activities.
- Mobilise women to form Self-Help Groups (SHGs).
- Encourage savings and utilise it for further income generation.
- Identifying local skills and utilise those skills in income generation and self-employment activities.
- Create income generating activities.
- Provide access to support services.
- Provide financial assistance.
- Provide technical assistance.
- Develop managerial capabilities.
- Encourage entrepreneurship.
- Provide training on innovative technologies.
- Give emphasis on improving women's control over material resources and strengthening economic security.
- Ensure equal wages for equal work.

In this direction NGOs can play a crucial role at the grassroot level. They can help rural women to form groups and work continuously with groups to make them strong, cohesive and sustainable.

Conclusion

The need of the hour is to create an environment which ensures dignity to the women, which could help her to overcome feelings of powerlessness so that she emerges the comforts of dependency and faces challenges of autonomy by enjoying her human rights. It necessitates that the situation of women be viewed in totality. A focus only on education or on economic independence may not necessarily solve the problem, it requires a change in attitude of the society including both men and women, cultural transformation and a paradigm shift in status of women. Non-governmental organisations involved in the task of women's emancipation and upliftment should also lay great stress on creating consciousness among the people to treat women at par in all walks of life. The government could lead a helping hand to their efforts. Now the time is ripe for government to have a fresh look on the existing legislations concerning women. Women's development movement has to be further intensified in order to function as watchdogs for the implementation of perspective plan for women and monitor the impact of various legal, social and economic measures taken or declared by the state. A multi-pronged effort need to be made on a relatively long term strategy so that even the poorest of the poor women become active participants in the national mainstream.

REFERENCES

Buch, Nirmala. 2001. "Panchayats and Women", *Employment News*, Vol. 26, No. 19.

Gopalan, Sarala and Mira Siva (eds.). 1999. "National Profile on Women, Health and Development in India", *Health for the Millions*, Vol. 25, No. 6.

Gupta, V.S. 2001. "Nation Building and Empowerment of Women", *Employment News*, Vol. 26, No. 19.

Khullar, K.K. 2001. "Women in the Indian National Movement", *Employment News*, Vol. 26, No. 19.

Mourya, O.P. 2001. "Occupational Pattern of Employment of Women in India and the World", *Employment News*, Vol. 26, No. 19.

Murugan, K.R. and Dharmalingam. 2000. "Self Help Groups—New Women's Movement in Tamil Nadu", *Social Welfare*, Vol. 47, No. 5.

Rishi Paul. 2001. "Environment Stress and Management: A Gender Specific Approach", *Kurukshetra*, Vol. 49, No. 8.

Shan, Vidyaben. 1997. "Women and the Market Economy", *Social Welfare*, Vol. 44, No. 1.

Sinha Archana and Shalu Nigam. 2000. "Time to Change Track?", *Social Welfare*, Vol. 47, No. 5.

Surea Kanthi, A. 2000. "Literacy—Essential for SHGs," *Social Welfare*, Vol. 47, No. 6.

Uma Devi, K. 2000. "Women's Education—What Direction?", *Social Welfare*, Vol. 47, No. 6.

Vaidya, Bankim Chandra V. 2002. "Some Aspects of Rural Development", *Kurukshetra*, Vol. 50, No. 6.

Vashistha, K.C. & Sasi Malik, 2002. "Some Strategic Efforts Towards Empowerment of Women", *University News*, Vol. 40, No. 5.

Women at a Glance. http://www.un.org.

6

Women Education

A Harbinger of Economic Development

Dr. Kalpana Sahu

Women constitute roughly half of the world's population. They are an integral part of the Indian Economy and have a great potentiality to contribute to the development of our country. Their capability and efficiency can be increased by means of education. This article proposes to ponder over the relation between women education and economic development. The rationale behind the study is that in the present scenario women are emerging as a source of power and symbol of peace and progress.

This article throws light on the various methods that have been evolved from time to time measure economic development. It has been widely acknowledged that human resource development is necessary for the speedy development of the nation. In this context education is vital because it provides an ideal society by giving vitality, vibrancy, strength and meaning to the learner's personality. So the paper seeks to highlight the importance of education in general and female education in particular.

Women constitute a large chunk of the population. To bring them into the production and development process it is imperative to equip them with education, training and knowledge. This article makes an attempt to prove that educated woman can help to overcome the obstacles that stand in the way of economic development.

Among the various pushing factors of educational development societal safeguard is one. So the paper makes a brief discussion of the steps taken by the govt. to promote female education. Finally the papers deals with concluding observations.

The paper is descriptive in nature. Books and journals are the main sources. Data have been collected from secondary sources. It is based on the hypothesis that educated woman contribute a lot to the economic prosperity of the country.

(I)

The concept of 'Economic Development' has attracted the attention of all since time immemorial. But economists in the past were mainly concerned with growth or with the problem of developed countries. Gradually people became conscious of the fact that 'Poverty anywhere is a threat to prosperity everywhere'. With that and especially after second world war attention was shifted to the problems of the developing countries. Mieer and Baldwin mentioned, "Maintaining development is a problem for rich countries but accelerating development is even more pressing matter for the poor countries".[1] They go to the extent of saying, "A study of the poverty of nations has even more urgency than a study of the wealth of nations".[2]

'Development' can be defined as "an increase in real income over a long period of time". Thus traditionally development was defined in economic terms. A sustained increase in GNP or GDP at the rate of 5 to 7 per cent per year was conceived as development. However this definition was rejected as the objectives of poverty elimination, reduction in economic inequality, employment generation, conservation of natural resources, etc. were not given due attention. Consequent upon the rejection of this narrow definition of economic development attempt was made to redefine the concept of economic development in terms of the reduction of poverty, inequality and unemployment in a growing economy. 'Redistribution with Growth' and 'Growth with Social Justice were

---

1. **W.C. Mitchell, 'Business Cycles', Quoted by Meier and Baldwin.**
2. **Meier and Baldwin, 'Economic Development, Theory, History and Policy'.**

the popular slogans. Charles P. Kindleberger and Bruce Herrick stated, "Economic development is defined to include improvements in material welfare, especially for persons with lowest incomes, the eradication of mass poverty, disease and early death, changes in the composition of inputs and outputs that generally include shifts in the underlying structure of production away from agricultural towards industrial activities, the organisation of the economy in such a way the productive employment in general among the working age population rather than the situation of a privileged minority; and correspondingly greater participation of broadly based groups in making decisions about the directions, economic and otherwise, in which they should improve their welfare".[3] The growing disenchantment with the GNP per capita has resulted in a number of alternative ways of measurement of development. One such measurement method known as physical quality of life index was constructed by D. Morris in 1979. This method emphasises quality of life as evidenced by the scale of literacy, life expectancy and infant mortality. Now-a-days we are interested more in sustainable development than in development alone. It calls for the conservation of resources which would make development sustainable without endangering the resources for future generations. Thus development means positive changes in socio-economic and cultural lives of majority of people on permanent basis without exploitation and violence. There are many prerequisites of economic development. Education or removal of illiteracy and ignorance is one of them.

(II)

Education is a powerful instrument that can effectively change, shape and mould society in a positive direction. It offers new dimensions in the lifestyle of individuals and prepare them as self-reliant and responsible members of society.[4] It acts as a liberating factor which helps man to come out of the clutches of materialism and to attain intellectual and spiritual consciousness. All people right from Sri Aurobindo-the prominent philosopher—

---

3. Charles P. Kindleberger and Bruce Herrick 'Economic Development'.
4. Anuradha Malik and Dr. Gourango Subudhi, 'Reading The Horse of Neo-Literacy, Literacy Mission Vol. XXI/No. 6.

down to Atal Bihari Vajpayee—attribute much importance to education. Sri Aurobindo remarked, "The past is our foundation, the present our material, the future our aim and Summit. Each must have its due and natural place in a national system of education".[5] Former Prime-Minister Atal Bihari Vajpayee stated, "a knowledge based society will enable us to leap frog in finding new and innovative ways to meet the challenges of building a just and equitable social order and seeking urgent solutions.[6] Education is considered as an important social infrastructure which helps in the development of human resource. It is labelled as the Panacea for social mobility and equality and as the only hope for the downtrodden.[7] Realising the importance of education the constitution of India made provision for free and compulsory education to children up to age of 14 years. During 1951-52 the percentage of India's educational expenditure to the Gross Domestic Product was 0.64 per cent. It became 4.11 per cent of the GDP during 2000-01.

When we come to speak of female education, its importance is great in the economic development of the country. The desire to have a knowledge based society can be fulfilled only by educating the females. Unless the light of knowledge dawn in the women folk of our country we can never join the community of developed nations. Mahatma Gandhi therefore rightly remarked "Educating a boy is the education of an individual but educating a woman is the education of the whole family." A woman equipped with the power of knowledge can contribute a lot to the development of the country.

(III)

The relation between woman education and development hardly needs to be underlined. That woman is a contributory factor of economic development can be proved by taking various things

5. **Dr. K. Venkatasubramanian, 'India as a Knowledge Society', Yojana– Vol. 47, Feb. 2003, No. 2.**
6. **Ibid.**
7. **Karuna Chanana, Treading the Hallowed Halls, Women in Higher Education in India EPW Vol. XXXV, No. 12.**

into consideration. Traditionally the role of woman was confined to child bearing and child rearing and to the maintenance of the family. Even then her role in the development process can not be ignored because it is she who enables the 'bread earner' i.e. the male person to become physically and mentally fit and to contribute to the production process. Women education leads to greater and better attention by mothers to the care of their children. The celebrated English poet remarked that the 'child is the father of man'. It may sound metaphoric but its truth is evident when we take the physical, mental and emotional development of a child. The natural desire of a child to grow into a healthy adult, free from hunger and malnutrition can be fulfilled by an educated working mother. A series of concerted efforts have been made for the well being of the children. The educated mothers, being aware of the benefits of these developmental programmes, help in their speedy implementation. Thus by properly taking care of the children an educated mother helps in the constitution of a sound labour force which is very important in the developmental process of the country.

Women education leads to greater participation of females in the labour market. They work in different spheres of the economy. Table—6.1 shows the employment of female work force in public and private sectors.

Table 6.1: Employment of Women in Organised Public and Private Sectors upto 2000

(in Lacs)

Year	*Public Sector*	*Private Sector*	*Total*
1971	8.60	10.80	19.40
1981	14.90	12.90	27.80
1991	23.40	14.30	37.70
1997	27.28	19.09	46.37
1999	28.11	20.18	48.29
2000	28.57	20.66	49.23

Source: Yojana March 2003.

The table shows a steady increase in the work participation rate of women. It causes an increase in the earning of the family which enables the children to get better education and training. With the advent of a highly mechanised era and automation in all fields, children need to be trained and educated to develop into skilled manpower. Since the number of jobs available in the market is decreasing, trained/skilled manpower is necessary to take up self-employment.[8]

Women education contributes to economic development by containing the growth of population or by means of the reduction in family size. An uneducated mother considers a child as the gift of god and is not very much conscious of the adverse impact of the increase in the size of the family. Fertility is demand determined rather than supply determined. Male and female earnings and educational level of parents are the determinants of demand for children. With the increase in male and female earnings the demand for children for economic reason (to earn extra income) diminishes. A child at this stage is considered a liability rather than an asset.

Women education is an important determinant of demand for children. An increase in education raises the proportion of women joining the labour force. The most widely accepted explanation for a positive correlation between women education and work participation is that education raises the productivity of time devoted to labour market more than that of time spent in home production. In other words, the opportunity cost of working in the home increases inducing women to work in the market.[9] The desire to have small number of children is more pronounced in the case of educated working mothers. More educated mothers spend more time in child care particularly in educational care. So they face a higher price of child care due to their high opportunity cost of time. Thus with the increase in the level of female literacy rate population growth is bound to be decline.

---

8. **Chandra Vanu, "A New Beginning' Literacy Mission, p. 12.**
9. **B.K. Vashist and R.K. Rana, "New Household Economics: Some Evidence in Support of it." "The Indian Economic Journal".**

There is positive correlation between women education and family income. Women education helps not only in the formation of better quality human capital but also in the formation of physical capital. With the increase in female education and with the reduction in family size family saving increases which leads to capital formation. Woman education, therefore, has immense significance as it has a vast role in determining socio-economic development.

(IV)

Realising the importance of female education, our constitution makers made some provisions in the preamble and in different articles of the constitution that came into force on 26th January 1950. Article 6.1 of the constitution laid stress on equality of opportunity for women and children in fields of education and employment. Article 15.3 says that nothing shall prevent the state from making any provision for women. Besides constitutional safeguards, various commissions and committees have been set up to promote female education. The university education commission of 1948-49 suggested to increase educational opportunities for women. The secondary education commission advised to make no distinction between education imparted to boys and girls. In 1959 the National Committee on Women's Education suggested to bridge the existing educational gulf between men and women within a very short period. Towards the end of the Five Year Plan (1961-66) the government set up a commission on education to link it with the programmes of national development. This committee endorsed the recommendations of the National Committee on Women's Education of 1959. The National Education Policy 1968 stated that the education of girls should receive emphasis not only on grounds of social justice but also because it accelerates social transformation. In view of the increasing gulf in the field of vocational education of policy suggested to organise ITIs and Polytechnic for women. The National Policy on Education of 1979 laid stress on giving incentives like mid-day meals, free text books, uniform, etc. for improving literacy among girls. Similarly the National Policy on Education, 1986, dealt specifically with the Education for Women's Equality. The National perspective plan, 1988-2000 reiterated to empower women through education. On 7th May 1990 a committee for the review of National Policy on Education (NPERC) was appointed. The committee recommended to give importance to gender equality, vocational training for women, research and development of women's studies, allocation of more resource in both plan and non-plan sectors of elementary, secondary, vocational and higher education.

Realising the fact that women are not merely the beneficiaries but also an integral part of development the policy planners accorded top priority to gender equality. The policies framed so far reaffirm the constitutional directives and helped to increase the literacy rate among females which is evident from Table—6.2.

Table 6.2: Percentage of Literate Women in India

Year	*Percentage of literacy among females*
1901	0.6
1911	1.1
1921	1.8
1931	2.9
1941	7.3
1951	7.9
1961	13.0
1971	18.7
1981	24.8
1991	39.4
1997	50.0

Source: University News, Vol. 38, Jan. 24, 2000 and Jan. 31, 2000.

In comparison to other states Orissa is lagging behind in the field of female education. Table—6.3 shows female literacy in Orissa.

Table 6.3: Literacy in Orissa (In per cent)

Year	*Total literacy*	*Male*	*Female*
1951	15.79	27.32	4.52
1961	21.66	34.68	8.65
1971	26.18	38.29	13.92
1981	34.23	47.09	21.12
1991	49.09	63.09	34.68

Source: Dhariti 20.6.2000.

(V)

Women education is very much necessary for the sustainable development of the country. The benefits of investment on female education will directly reflect on the economic development and efficiency of a nation. Educated, healthy, enlightened and empowered women are very much essential for the achievement and maintenance of economic development. To hardness their potentiality, more and more incentives are to be given. A major drawback of women education is drop-outs and stagnation which is evident in Table—6.4.

Table 6.4: Drop-out Rates for the Year 1997-98 (In per cent)

Class	*Girls*
I-V	41.34
I-VIII	58.61
I-X	72.67

Source: Annual Report 1998-99, MHRD, department of Education GOI, 1999.

Preventive measures for the increasing drop-out problem are urgently needed. In the post-liberalisation era, government support to education has been reduced. Private sector is allowed to enter into this field. The cost of education becomes very high. It is apprehended that the share of women in education is likely to receive a set back. Time has come to give a second thought to the problem.

REFERENCES

1. W.C. Mitchel, '*Business Cycles*', Quoted by Meier and Baldwin.
2. Meier and Baldwin, '*Economic Development, Theory, History and Policy*.
3. Charles P. Kindleberger and Bruce Herrick, '*Economic Development*'.
4. Literacy Mission Vol. XXI/No. 6.
5. Yojana- Vol. 47, Feb. 2003.
6. EPW Vol. XXXV.
7. Indian Economic Journal, Vol. 37, April-June 1990, No. 4.
8. B.N. Pande, '*On Development and National Integration*'.
9. R.K. Kekhi, '*The Theories of Development and Planning*'.

7

Women Education and Development in Orissa

A Paradigm Shift

Dr. A.S.C. Patnaik

Introduction

In the present day fast moving world, women are seen taking active part in every field of work—agriculture to industry and space research. Today, we witness women in every walk of our daily life, working actively in some job or the other, struggling for the development of the nation. Realising the importance of women's role in the present day society and nation building—the present research study on women education and development has been conducted taking all necessary secondary data, since last five years into consideration.

Basically the economy of India is rural in nature and in India nearly 77 per cent of population reside in villages. Ours is an agricultural economy and hence we cannot think of rural women's education and their development, ignoring the Government help for them. Active Government participation with different educational programmes and promotional schemes to impart primary education, are vital for the upliftment of women's education in rural India.

Object and Scope

In this chapter, the researcher has tried to highlight the role of Government of Orissa for the education of women in the state.

Different educational programmes of Government of Orissa have been intensively studied and analysed in the present study. For the purpose of the study the researcher used the necessary secondary sources of data since last 5 years. All the limitations of secondary data are also found in this study.

Educational Programmes of the Government—At a Glance

The important educational programmes taken up by Government of Orissa for the education and development of women at primary level are as follows:

1. Early Childhood Care Education (ECCE)
2. Universalisation of Elementary Education (UEE)
3. District Primary Education Programme (DPEP)
4. Sarba Sikhya Abhijan (SSA)
5. Mass Education Programme (MEP)
6. Education Guarantee Scheme (EGS)

Besides the primary educational programmes, Government of Orissa has actively taken the following higher education programmes for the development of women in Orissa.

1. Secondary stage of education (classes VIII to X) under Board of Secondary Education, Orissa.
2. Computer Education in High Schools.
3. Higher Secondary Education regulated by the Council of Higher Secondary Education, Orissa.
4. Vocational Education.
5. Teachers Education and Training.
6. Technical Education and Training.

For the present study, education and development programmes for women at primary education level is taken into consideration.

Education and Development Programmes for Women in Orissa—A Review

The Indian population has increased three folds from 33 crores in 1947 during the year of independence to 102.7 crores by

March, 2001. The literacy rate in general has gone up by about 25 per cent and about 50 per cent of the male population and 35 per cent of female population have become literates. Further the gap between the literacy of males and females has also reduced significantly.

The per capita income of Orissa has increased at a diminishing rate. It was Rs. 6806/- during the year 1995-96 and Rs. 8547/- in the year 2000-01. Most of the people of Orissa are below the poverty line i.e. 47.2 per cent in the year 1999-2000. The position of Orissa in various fields in the country is explained in the Table—7.1.

Table 7.1: The Position of Orissa and its Growth in Various Fields

State	*Education*	*Health*	*Agriculture*	*Investment*	*Low*	*Overall growth*
AP	13	11	04	10	11	10
WB	14	12	10	17	16	14
Bihar	19	16	16	19	19	18
Orissa	15	18	18	18	13	19

Source: The Samaj, 19th Oct. 2003.

In education, the rate of Orissa is at 15th rank and in overall growth it is at 19th position.

The Constitution of India casts an obligation on the state of Orissa to provide free and compulsory education to all children upto the age of 14 years. The literacy rate in Orissa during the year 1951 was 15.8 per cent against the all India average of 18.3 per cent which increased to 63.08 per cent during the year 2001 against the all India average of 64.8 per cent. While the male literacy rate is 63.1 per cent in the state during 1991 has increased to 75.95 per cent during 2001, the female literacy rate has increased from 34.7 per cent to 50.51 per cent. There is a steady improvement in the literacy rates of the state over successive decades, due to the expansion of educational infrastructure both in qualitative and quantitative.

During the year 1950-51, there were 9801 Primary Schools with 16,525 teachers and 3.15 lakh students, 501 Upper Primary

Schools with 2,569 teachers and 40,000 students and 172 High Schools with 2,247 teachers and 16,000 students respectively.

Early Childhood Care Education (ECE)

The UNICEF assisted ECE programme is being implemented in the state during 1982 with the objective of motivating children in the age group of 3-5 years towards primary education with a view to achieve the Universalisation of Elementary Education (UEE). Motivation of pre-school children by programmes like the use of Play-material, and developing basic learning material have been done by institutions set up under ECE programme. ICDS Projects and agencies like State Council of Child Welfare Advisory Board are continuously administering the primary education through Anganwadis, Balwadis and Creche centres.

Elementary Education

Once of the component of "Basic Minimum Service" of the Government is "Universalisation of Elementary Education". The strategy of UEE covers three aspects of elementary education i.e. (i) Universal access and enrolment, (ii) Universal retention of children upto 14 years of age, and (iii) Substantial improvement in the quality of education to enable all children to achieve essential level of learning. This lead to expansion of primary as well as upper primary education in the Govt. sector, especially in the rural India.

The state provides primary schools within one kilometer and upper primary schools within three kilometers from habitations having a population of 300 or 300+ and 500 and 500+ respectively. The position of Elementary Education in Orissa since 1999-00 to 2003-04 is given in the following Table—7.2.

Table 7.2: Number of Primary Schools, Enrolment of Students and Teachers in Orissa

Sl. No.	*Item*	*1999-00*	*2000-01*	*2001-02*	*2002-03*	*2003-04*
1	*2*	*3*	*4*	*5*	*6*	*7*
1.	Primary Schools (in Nos.)	65,552	65,552	42,824	42,824	44,416
(i)	Formal	42,104	42,104	42,824	42,824	44,416
(ii)	Non-formal	23,448	23,448	–	–	–

(Table Contd...)

1	2	3	4	5	6	7
2.	Enrolment (in '000)	5,232	5,296	4,769	4,824	5,254
(i)	Formal	4,646	4,710	4,769	4,824	5,254
(ii)	Non-formal	586	586	–	–	–
3.	Teachers (in Nos.)	1,35,384	1,39,135	1,16,231	83,652	97,175
(i)	Formal	1,11,040	1,14,791	1,16,231	83,652	97,175
(ii)	Non-formal	24,344	24,344	–	–	–

Source: Director, Elementary Education, Bhubaneswar, Orissa (2003-04) p. 2.

During 2003-04, 44,416 primary schools with 52.54 lakh enrolment and 0.97 lakh teachers were functioning in the state. There was one primary school for every 3.5 km. area. The teacher-student ratio during 2003-04 was 1 : 54.

Further to boost primary education in Orissa, it has been proposed to open 325 primary schools and to appoint 15000 Swecha Sevi Sikhya Sahayaks (para-teachers) during the year 2004-05. The present 9209 Swecha Sevi Sikhya Sahayaks will be continued during 2004-05. An amount of Rs. 14.95 crore has been spent during 2004-05 for the purpose.

Since 1990-91, Government has taken steps for providing basic infrastructure, including school buildings under the Operation Black Board Programme in rural Orissa. During 1991-92 to 2002-03, 12,421 primary school buildings were constructed involving an expenditure of Rs. 175.12 crore. In 2003-04, 47 school buildings have been completed under OBB involving an expenditure of Rs. 0.28 crore.

Government of Orissa introduced a Mid-Day Meal Programme from 1995, July with a view to increase retention of elementary school children and to reduce the drop out rates. In 2003-04, 46.32 lakh children in 51,931 schools were covered under this programme. Under this programme 16.39 lakh children were provided cooked food and 29.93 lakh children were provided with dry ration. These 46.32 lakh children belong to the schools under Schools and Mass Education Department as well as NLEP Schools and Special Schools of Women and Child Development Department and schools under ST and SC Development Department.

The drop out rate at the primary stage was 33.6 per cent, while the drop out rate of girls and boys are 35.4 per cent and 31.9 per cent respectively during 2003-04 as against 34.2 per cent, 36.5 per cent and 32.3 per cent respectively during the previous year i.e. 2002-03. The drop out rate among SC and ST students, which was 37.2 per cent and 53.3 per cent respectively during 2002-03 had declined to 35.5 and 52.1 per cent respectively during 2003-04 which is explained in Table—7.3.

Table 7.3: Drop out Rate in Primary Schools during 2000-01 to 2003-04 in Orissa

	All category			*Scheduled Castes*			*Scheduled Tribes*		
Years	*Boys*	*Boys*	*Boys*	*Boys*	*Girls*	*Girls*	*Total*	*Girls*	*Total*
1	2	3	4	5	6	7	8	9	10
2000-01	42.3	41.1	41.8	50.5	54.3	52.0	61.7	66.5	63.4
2001-02	42.0	40.0	41.0	50.0	52.0	51.0	61.0	65.0	63.0
2002-03	32.3	36.5	34.2	35.8	38.7	37.2	49.3	57.4	53.3
2003-04	31.9	35.4	33.6	34.6	36.6	35.5	48.2	56.6	52.1

Source: Economic Survey, Bhubaneswar, Orissa, 2003-04, p. 14/3.

District Primary Education Programme (DPEP)

This programme was launched in the year 1996-97 in Orissa to achieve the goal of universalisation of primary education through district specific programme. The basic objectives of the DPEP scheme are as follows:

1. Providing access to primary education for all children.
2. Reducing the drop-out rate to less than 10 per cent.
3. Increasing learning achievement of primary school children by 25 per cent.
4. Reducing the gap among gender and disadvantaged social groups to less than 5 per cent.

The DPEP has been conducted in two phases. In each phase eight districts were covered with a project cost of Rs. 313.80 crores in Orissa.

At the end of the year 2003-04, 1,578 new primary schools have been opened for boys and girls in all districts of Orissa, with enrolment of 50,697 students and 5,775 para-teachers. In DPEP Programme 42 lakh free text books have been distributed among the students. The gender gap proved a remarkable decrease as more girl students enrolled in DPEP schools.

Sarba Sikhya Abhijan (SSA)

It is a nation wide programme to achieve constitutional goal of universalisation of elementary education and to provide useful and quality education to all children in the age group of 6-14 years by 2010.

The objectives of the programme are as follows:

1. All children of 6-14 years age group to be in schools by 2003.
2. All children to complete 5 years of schooling by 2007.
3. All children to complete 8 years of schooling by 2010.
4. Universal Retention by 2010.
5. Bridge all gender and social gaps at primary level by 2007 and at upper primary level by 2010.
6. Infrastructure improvement in schools.

The scheme is implemented in all districts of Orissa during 2003-04 and the achievements studied are as follows:

1. During the year 2003-04, 780 new primary schools and 2771 new U.P. schools were opened for out-of-school children.
2. All Government schools were provided a grant of Rs. 2,000/- for school improvement and Rs. 5,000/- for repairs and maintenance per annum during 2003-04.
3. Free text books were supplied to 41,83,039 SC, ST and girls students reading in Primary and U.P. schools at a cost of Rs. 16.56 crores.
4. All the 84,221 primary school teachers and 42,533 U.P. school teachers were given teaching and learning material grant of Rs. 500/- during the year 2003-04.

Besides these, during the year 2003-04, 30 Block Resource Centre buildings, 90 Duster Resource Centre buildings, 66 new Primary Schools, 867 new U.P. School buildings and 169 buildings for building less U.P. schools have been constructed. At the same time additional class rooms to 4180 schools, drinking water facilities to 1388 primary schools, electrification in 100 schools and boundary walls in 21 schools have been completed. Four hundred special hostels have been opened for ST girl students and 63000 ST students have been given the bilingual primers during the year 2003-04.

Mass Education Programme

The Mass Education Programme, as a part of National Literacy Mission (NIM), was introduced in the state in the year 1991-92 with an objective to educate the non-literate woman and men of 15-35 age group. As the state level, the State Literacy Mission Authority (SLMA) and the Zilla Sakhyarata Samiti (ZSS) at the district level are the implementing agencies of the programme. Out of 67 lakh non-literates in the age group 15-35 covering all the districts in the state, about 30 lakh could be made literates during 1991-2001 and the remaining 37 lakh are expected to be covered under the scheme of Total Literacy Campaign (TLC), Post Literacy Programme (PLP) and the Continuing Education Programme (CEP) during the coming decade. TLC and PLP activities as on 31st March, 2004 since inception is given in the Table—7.4.

Table 7.4: Purpose of Expenditure for Mass Education Programme

Sl. No.	*Activities*	*Amount released (Rs. in Crs.)*	*Expenditure (Rs. in Crs.)*	*No. of persons covered (in lakhs)*	
				Total	*Females*
1	2	3	4	5	6
1.	Total Literacy Campaign (TLC)	38.65	35.37	35.50	19.88
2.	Post Literacy Programme (PLP)	14.69	13.78	19.31	10.79

Source: Director, Elementary Education, Bhubaneswar, 2004, p. 10.

In the State Plan, a sum of Rs. 100 lakh has been proposed for TLC programme in the year 2004-05.

Education Guarantee Scheme (EGS)

It is a centrally sponsored scheme with 75 : 25 sharing between the Centre and the State, was introduced during 2001-02 in the place of former Non-formal Education, to provide primary school education.

By the end of the year 2003-04, 19,009 EGS centres including 1606 centres under NGOs have been opened providing access and enrolment to 5,96,326 children in the age group of 6-14 years. The Alternative and Innovative Education Programme (AIE) which is a component of EGS for marginalised and deprived groups of children because of household work, migration, religious beliefs and customs, engagement in economic activity, extreme poverty, etc. has also been adopted by State Government for implementation. By the end of 2003-04, 355 AIE centres have been opened in the State with an enrolment of 10,944 boys and girls students.

Upper Primary Schools—At a Glance

The number of U.P. schools by the end of 2003-04 were 14,233. The following table shows the number of U.P. Schools, enrolment and number of teachers for the period from 1999-00 to 2003-04 is explained in the Table—7.5.

Table 7.5: No. of U.P. Schools, Enrolment and Teachers

S. No.	*Item*	*1999-00*	*2000-01*	*2001-02*	*2002-03*	*2003-04*
1.	No. of U.P. Schools (middle schools)	12,406	12,406	11,510	11,510	14,233
2.	Enrolment ('000)	1,412	1,057	1,055	1,182	1,233
3.	No. of Teachers	40,706	40,706	38,914	41,375	49,786

Source: Economic Survey, Bhubaneswar, Orissa, 2003-04, p. 14/7.

The drop out rates in U.P. Schools in Orissa is shown in the Table—7.6.

Table 7.6: **Dropout Rates in Upper Primary Schools in Orissa**

Years	*All Category*			*Scheduled Castes*			*Scheduled Tribes*		
	Boys	*Boys*	*Boys*	*Boys*	*Girls*	*Girls*	*Total*	*Girls*	*Total*
1	*2*	*3*	*4*	*5*	*6*	*7*	*8*	*9*	*10*
2000-01	52.9	61.1	57.0	49.7	69.7	58.6	70.9	77.1	73.0
2001-02	52.0	60.5	56.0	49.0	68.0	58.0	70.0	76.0	73.0
2002-03	57.7	60.5	59.0	45.7	49.2	47.5	75.0	80.3	77.7
2003-04	56.5	58.6	57.5	60.9	65.3	63.0	73.0	78.5	75.6

Source: Economic Survey, Bhubaneswar, Orissa, 2003-04, p. 14/7.

The dropout rate at upper primary stage during the year 2002-03 was 59 per cent which has been decreased to 57.5 per cent during 2003-04. The drop out rate of girls all these years is more than boys in general category as well as S.C. category but less in ST category. The drop out of girls was 60.5 per cent during 2002-03 and reduced to 58.6 per cent in the year 2003-04 under general category. The drop out of girls in SC category was 49.2 per cent during the year 2002-03 and decreased to 65.3 per cent during the year 2003-04. There was heavy drop out rate in S.T. category i.e. 80.3 per cent during 2002-03, which reduced to 78.5 per cent during 2003-04 which proved a remarkable achievement.

Conclusion and Suggestions

The scenario of women education and development is quite encouraging, as the drop out rates of girls in all categories, SC, ST in primary schools has alarmingly decreased during 2000-01 to 2003-04 period.

In Upper Primary School Education the drop out rate of girls during 2000-01 to 2003-04 has decreased to a little extent in general category, first decreased and then increased in SC category girls and first increased and then decreased in the ST category girls during the same period.

Moreover, there is a decreasing trend in the number of primary schools; number of teachers in these schools and student's enrolment since 1999-00 to 2002-03.

The rate of drop out of girls is more than boys in primary schools in Orissa during 2002-03 in General, SC and ST categories. It is found, the girls in villages are extensively preoccupied with household works, engaged in farms, and economic activities due to extreme poverty etc.

At last it is concluded, as more and more girls are encouraged by Government schemes to attend primary schools, the drop out rates gradually show a declining trend.

Suggestions

1. Government of Orissa should take necessary steps to provide one Primary School within 1 km. for maximum villages in the state, for healthy women education at least upto primary stage.
2. Government should improve its Mid Day Meal Programme—Cooked meal and Dry ration schemes according to the needs of the primary school children, so that the drop outs will be decreased.
3. Free Educational study materials like text books, pencils etc. should be supplied in Primary Schools.
4. More advertisements regarding the benefits of education through colourful hoardings at the site of schools will attract children for education. For maximising enrolments Heads of villages should be motivated. Different marketing and promos may be used tactfully for the improvement of women education in Orissa.
5. Injecting more and more Swechha Sevi Sikhya Sahayaks in primary education improve women education and development in a better way.
6. Elderly men and women should be convinced properly, the benefits of educating their children.
7. Lastly, everyone must understand, "Educating a Woman Means Educating a Family".

REFERENCES

1. Economic Survey, Govt. of Orissa, Bhubaneswar, 2003-04.
2. The Journal of Commerce and Economics, Berhampur, Orissa, Vol. XIII, 2004.
3. Director's Report, Elementary Education, Orissa, Bhubaneswar, 2003-04.

8

Women Education and Development

P.K. Chhotroy

Women in India stand to-day on the threshold of a new era in their endeavour to become full citizens assured of human rights and dignity. They seek an integration into the national mainstream as equal partners in progress and development. Socio-economic advancement of a country can be best judged by the status and position which it can bestow on its women. The size of female population in India indicates the potential strength of women in the total human resource of the country. Women contribute much time and energy to keep the nation going. Their contribution to the economic growth of the society is quite substantial. As Jackson H (1998) says, "A Woman who created and sustains a home and through whose heads children grow up to be strong and pure men and women, is a creator second only to God. To Gandhiji "Women is the companion of men gifted with equal mental capacities. She has the right to participate in all walks of life along with men. She has the same right of freedom and liberty as men's. She is entitled to a supreme place in her own sphere of activity as man is." Jhabvala (1984) says; "Money in the hands of a men spend quite differently from money in hands of a women." An ILO study finds that men tend to spend 60 per cent of their income in their home and 40 per cent on themselves, where as a women spends 90 per cent of her income on her family and only 10 per cent on herself. Thus, when a women controls the household income the family gets more benefits. In India, women constitute slightly less than 50 per cent of the country's population. Despite some favourable traditional values and customs and emergence of powerful women personalities down the ages, women are discriminated against in practically all walks of life. After independence it was realised that India's potential can not be harnessed unless women became equal partner in development.

Human Development and Economic Growth

The issues relating to human development have come to the fore in the last few decades because of the fact that the benefits of economic growth do not necessarily accrue to all sections of the community automatically. The ultimate objective of social and economic changes is human development. Human development has been described as a process of enlarging human capabilities and choices. Apart from the basic necessities such as food, clothing and shelter, other human choices include long life, good health, adequate education and participative decision making. Thus, human development is multi-dimensional involving political, social and economic elements. It is not, therefore, surprising that countries do not rank identifically on the income scale and human development scale. Some times the differences in the ranking are quite striking. A development strategy focused on human development seeks, therefore, to ensure for as large a section of the society as possible an acceptable standard of living. Human development in any country can be seen as the result of benefits flowing from the stock of capital that the country possesses. In the broadest sense of the term, a country's capital comprises:

(i) *Natural capital:* natural resources including atmosphere and oceans, flora, fauna, soils, mineral deposits and sources of fresh water.

(ii) *Physical capital:* produced means of production, i.e. plant and equipments, physical infrastructure (e.g. roads, bridges and irrigation canals), stock of dwellings, etc.; and

(iii) *Human capital:* knowledge, skills, experience, energy and inventiveness of people acquired in a variety of ways including formal education, training on the job learning by doing, informal contacts, information media, and reflection.

Enhancing human development means augmenting the stock of capital—natural, physical and human. Human Development Report 1995 highlights the four main components of the human development paradigm:

(a) *Productivity:* People must be enabled to increase their productivity and to participate fully in the process of income generation and remunerative employment. Economic growth is, therefore, a subset of human development models.

(b) *Equity:* People must have access to equal opportunities. All barriers to economic and political opportunities must be eliminated so that people can participate in, and benefit from, these opportunities.

(c) *Sustainability:* Access to opportunities must be ensured not only for the present generations but for future generations as well. All forms of capital—physical, human, environmental—should be replenished.

(d) *Empowerment:* Development must be by people, not only for them people must participate fully in the decisions and processes that shape their lives. For this, an appropriate political and social framework becomes necessary.

Human development implies economic growth. Sustained improvement in human well being is not possible without economic growth but, at the same time, high economic growth need not necessarily translate into higher levels of human development. Studies have shown that economic growth requires effective policy management if it is to enrich human development. Conversely, if human development is to be durable, it must be continuously supported by economic growth. Any imbalance between the creation of capabilities in people which is what human development aims to achieve and the absorption of these capabilities in productive activities which is what economic growth can result in, can create social upheaval. Wastage of human resources can be most detrimental to any society. Human development has therefore, to go hand in hand with economic growth.

Human Capital Formation

In Economics, it was thought for a long time that it was a physical capital which played a crucial part in expanding production. In recent years, a new concept of "Human capital" has been evolved and emphasised. The term "Human capital formation" refers to the process of acquiring and increasing the number of persons who have skills, education and experience which are critical for economic and political development of a country. Human capital formation is thus associated with investment in man and his development as a creative and productive resource (Harbison, 1962).

In its wider sense, investment in human capital means expenditure on health education and social services in general and its narrower sense it implies expenditure on education and training. Mehta (1976) rightly says that a rapid rate of human capital formation is as important a precondition for economic growth as the rapid rate of physical capital formation.

Studies made by Schultz, Harbison, Denisan, Kendrick, Abramovitz, Becker, Bowman, Kuznets and a host of other economists reveal that one of the important facts responsible for the rapid growth of American economy has been the relatively increasing outlays on education. They tell us that a dollar invested in education brings a greater increase in national income than a dollar spent on dams, roads, factories or other tangible capital goods. In Galbraith's words "We now get the larger part of our industrial growth not from more capital investment but from investment in man and improvements brought about by improved men." Even earlier, economists like Adam Smith, Veblen and Marshall stressed the importance of human capital in production. The level and rate of economic growth depend on natural resources, physical capital accumulation, human resource development and technological progress, provided the socio-cultural environment is favourable to growth. Capital and natural resources and passive factors of production, human beings are the active agents who accumulate capital, exploit natural resources, build social, economic and political organisations and carry forward national development. Clearly, a country which is unable to develop the skill and knowledge of its people and utilise them effectively in the national economy will be unable to develop anything else.

Human Capital Indicators

For the purpose of international comparisons, the following indicators of the stock of human capital would be useful:

(1) Level of educational attainment; and (2) the number of persons, expressed as a percentage of population of the labour force, which is engaged in high level occupations, like scientists, engineers, managers, teachers, doctors, scientific and engineering technicians, nurses and medical assistants and persons in the foreman and skilled worker category. The "second best" measures, indicating the growth of HCF universally recognised, (i) the number of teachers (primary and secondary levels) per 10,000 population; (ii) engineers and scientists per 10,000 population; (iii) physicians and dentists per 10,000 population, (iv) pupils enrolled at the primary levels as a percentage of the estimated population in the corresponding age-group; (v) the adjusted school enrolment ratio for primary and secondary levels combined; (vi) pupils enrolled at the secondary level as a percentage of the estimated population in the corresponding age-group; and (vii) enrolment at the higher level as a percentage of the population in the corresponding age-group. The first three are partial measures of the stock of human resources and the next four are measures of addition to it.

Strategies for Human Capital Formation

The following are the main strategies:

(a) Enrichment of primary education with the help of educational technology; (b) Universalisation of primary education; (c) Compulsory and free education upto 14 years; (d) Importance of vocational or craft education at the higher secondary level; (e) Making school education more effective with appropriate teaching technology; (f) Improving quality of teacher education; (g) Making non-formal education to keep up with the fast changing world; (h) Checking population explosion; (i) Starting multipurpose schools; (j) Encouraging science and technical education; (k) Promoting rapid industrialisation and using indigenous technology; (l) Giving priority to research institutes for all faculties.

Social Sector Development

The publication of the National Human Development Report 2001 by the Planning Commission earlier in March this year would, by all means, be considered a land mark step towards giving new direction to the process of development during the Tenth Five Year Plan. The report focuses on the issues of governance for human development. The Deputy Chairman, Planning Commission, Shri K.C. Pant rightly points out in the foreward to the Report: Human Development has to reflect and address the social concerns and processes that underline the various outcomes. It has to also recognise the local constraints and aspirations of the people. The Foreward also points out that process of development should be assessed in terms of what it does for an average individual and adds: The process of development has to be seen in terms of the benefits and opportunities that it generates for people and how these are eventually distributed—between men and women, the well off and deprived and across regions. Experience shows that, often, there is no direct correspondence between economic attainments of a society and the quality of life.

The term social sector is often used to refer to education, health and nutrition sectors. According to K. Seeta Prabhu, Head, Human Development Resource Centre at the UNDP, India Country Office, the term has not been formally defined and thus has come to acquire several connotations. One of the definitions of social sectors is related to human development as against human resource development. The UNDP defines Human Development Approach as the process of enlarging people's choices. The concept encompasses empowerment cooperation, equity in basic capabilities and opportunities, sustainability and security. In this approach, people occupy centre stage and measures such as education, health and nutrition are emphasised for their intrinsic value and their role in enhancing the basic capabilities of people. The emergence of the concept of human development can be traced to efforts by economists such as Amartya Sen who defines standard of living in terms of functioning and capabilities rather than in terms of commodity possessions. This approach emphasises acquisition of education, health and nutrition, which is considered as an essential human rights. However, in the Approach paper the social infrastructure segment includes education, health and nutrition in addition to rural water supply. The document rationalises the premise of social development by including rural water supply under the social infrastructure as drinking water problem is a governance issue and has a bearing on the quality of life, that large majority of people in the rural areas experience every day.

Education

In terms of human development objectives, education is an end in itself, not just a means to an end. Education, which is basic human right, is critical for economic and social development. It is crucial for building human capabilities and for opening opportunities. Without education, development can be neither broad based nor sustained.

Amartya Sen and Jean Dreze in one of their books—India Economic Development and Social Opportunity, point out that education and health can be seen to be valuable to the freedom of a person in at least five distinct ways:

- *Intrinsic importance:* Being educated and healthy are valuable achievements in themselves, and the opportunity to have them can be of direct importance to a person's effective freedom.
- *Instrumental personal roles:* A person's education and health can help him or her to do many things—other than just being educated and healthy—that are also valuable. They can, for instance, be important for getting a job and more generally for making use of economic opportunities.
- *Instrumental social roles:* Greater literacy and basic education can facilitate public discussion of social needs and encourage informed collective demands. These in turn can help expand the facilities that the public enjoys, and contribute to the better utilization of the available services.

- *Instrumental process roles:* The process of schooling can have benefits even aside from its explicitly aimed objectives, namely formal education. For example, the incidence of child labour is intimately connected with non-schooling of children, and the expansion of schooling can reduce the distressing phenomenon of child labour so prevalent in India. Schooling also brings young people in touch with others and thereby broadens their horizons.
- *Empowerment and distributive roles:* Greater literacy and educational achievements of disadvantaged groups can increase their ability to resist oppression, to organise politically, and to get a fairer deal.

Economic growth cannot be the only objective for national planning and indeed over the years, development objectives are being defined not just in terms of increases in GDP or per capita income but broader in terms of enhancement of human well-being. This includes not only an adequate level of consumption of food and other types of consumer goods but also access to basic social services especially education, health, availability of drinking water and basic sanitation. It also includes expansion of economic and social opportunities for all individuals and groups, reduction in disparities, and greater participation in decision-making. The Tenth Plan must set suitable targets in these areas to ensure significant process towards improvement in the quality of life of all our people.

Women's Education: Still A Distant Dream

Education, specially for women, is an important agent of socialisation, and instrument of social transformation, and a channel of social mobility and equality. Education of girls and women has to be a universal movement for their empowerment, for changing current stereo-typed and replacing the existing structures. Women are the agents of change. Education is considered a key instrument for this change, which is responsible for national development. It is true to the saying, "If you educate a boy you educate an individual, but it you educate a girl, you educate a family, society and ultimately the nation." But the changes in our society are slow, it is because we have still not allowed our woman to play their active role in the society which by nature they are most suitable to do.

Education liberates women from ignorance and enhances their self esteem. It enables them to choose their own way and look after their families in a better way. Napolean has rightly said, Give me an educated mother, I shall promise you the birth of a civilized nation." The Education commission's report rightly observed "The destiny of India is being shaped in her classroom."

Women's education bring about more awareness. Educated mothers becomes more knowledgeable and vigilant enhancing their ability to rear and bring up children in a better way. There is a positive correlation between women literacy rate and life expectancy. While illiteracy is invariably associated with poverty, malnutrition, deprivation, high mortality, high population growth and all other aspects of underdevelopment, women's education become imperative.

The revised National Educational Policy (1986) part IV, entitled "Education for Equality" says that:

(i) Education will be used as an agent of basic change in the status of women in order to neutralise the accumulated distortions of the past. It will foster the development of new values through redesigned curriculum, text books, the training and active involvement of educational institutions.

(ii) In the removal of women's literacy and obstacles inhibiting their access to and retention in elementary education. Major emphasis will be given on women's participation in vocational technical and professional education at different levels and effective monitoring is also taken into consideration.

Our constitution directs clearly that, efforts should be made for equality in educational opportunities irrespective of sex, religion, caste and social or economic status. But, this is far from being reality. Even after fifty eight years of independence there still exists a great disparity between the level of male and female education.

Empowerment of women is directly linked with education. It is unfortunate that even after five decades of independence we have not been able to combat illiteracy, which ultimately leads to poverty. The 1991 census shows that India is 52.21 per cent literate. Among them 64.13 per cent are males and 39.29 per cent females. The 2001 census shows that the percentage of literacy for men and women is 75.9 per cent and 54.2 per cent respectively. Table—8.1 shows literacy rates from 1951 to 1991 (Sex-wise).

In spite of considerable improvement in health, education and employment sectors, women still comprise the largest section of population living in absolute poverty and they represent poorest of the poor.

Table 8.1: Percentage of Literacy Rate in India 1951-1991

Year	*Male*	*Female*	*Person*
1951	27.16	8.86	18.33
1961	40.40	15.34	28.31
1971	45.95	21.97	34.45
1981	53.45	28.46	41.42
1981*	56.37	29.75	43.56
1991	64.13	39.29	52.21
Rural Combined	57.87	30.62	44.69
Urban	81.09	64.05	73.08

* Relates to population 7 years and above comparable with 2001.

Source: Census of India, 2001.

Women not only continue to be in marginal employment and low levels of skills, their contribution continue to be 'invisible.'

Lack of education, training and low level of literacy not merely excluded woman from social, economic and political power but knowledge power as well. Therefore, while comprising half of the humanity "contributing 2/3rd of the world's work hours, she earns only 1/3rd of the total income and owns less than 1/10th of the world resources."

An NCERT study found that the states where the primary stage constituted classes I-IV the dropout rate of girls was very high and even higher amongst rural girls. Educational statistics of MHRD group of India (1988-89), also indicate that drop outs between classes I-VIII was 60.70 per cent for boys and 70.05 per cent for girls. But the percentage of girls drop out has decreased considerably during the decade 1991-2001.

No country can strive to prosper and develop when a large proportion of its female population continues to remain illiterate and backward.

Reallocation of Public Sector Resources

Human Development Report 1991 (UNDP) introduced for expenditure ratios which are considered necessary to "analyse" how public spending on human development can be designed and monitored".

(i) *the Public Expenditure Ratio (PER):* the percentage of national income that goes into public expenditure;

(ii) *the Social Allocation Ratio (SAR):* the percentage of public expenditures earmarked for social services;

(iii) *the Social Priority Ratio (SPR):* the percentage of social expenditure devoted to human priority concerns (i.e., say, elementary education, preventive health care, nutrition, water supply and sanitation); and

(iv) *the Human Expenditure Ratio (HER):* the percentage of national income devoted to human priority concerns; the last one being the product of the first three ratios.

[HER = PER × SAR × SPR,

since

$$\frac{HPE}{NY} = \left(\frac{PE}{NY}\right) \times \left(\frac{SS}{PE}\right) \times \left(\frac{HPE}{SS}\right)$$

The Report provided norms for the various ratios, the fulfilment of which is expected to lead to higher levels of human development—the norms being derived from the experience of a number of countries in respect of human development.

According to the Report, the Human Expenditure Ratio (HER) may need to be around 5 per cent of a country wishes to do well in human development. This may be achieved in an efficient manner by keeping "the Public Expenditure Ratio (PER) moderate (around 25 per cent), allocate much of this to the social sectors (more than 40 per cent) and focus on social priority areas (giving them more than 50 per cent)." The Report however adds, "what probably matters more than the HER is human development spending per person in absolute terms. This helps place the ratio in proper perspective." This approach has been criticized to some extent on the grounds that it implies that all human development expenditure is financed by Government out of taxation or borrowings, which is neither correct nor desirable.

While public expenditure ratios do provide a clue to the seriousness of effort made, they themselves do not fully explain the level of human development in a country. Much depends on the efficiency with which the resources allocated are utilised. Leakages and inefficiencies are endemic in such expenditures, plugging of which becomes essential, if the full benefits of such expenditures are to be reaped.

In an empirical study of 9 countries (India, Zambia, Jamaica, Pakistan, Egypt, Sri Lanka, Tunisia, Mexico and the Philippines), Giovanni and Stewart (1993, 'Two Errors of Targeting', UNICEF, International Child Development Centre, Florence, Italy, Innocenti Occasional Papers, EPS 36, March as quoted in Griffin and McKinley (1994), 'Implementing a Human Development Strategy' Macmillan) examine two common mistakes that occur while targeting public expenditure on specific groups:

1. *E-mistakes:* occur when there is excessive coverage of the population i.e., when people not intended to be included among the beneficiaries nonetheless receive benefits.

2. *F-mistakes:* occur when persons who are intended to be beneficiaries nonetheless fail to be covered by the programme and hence fail to receive benefits.

Policy makers often concentrate on minimizing the E-mistakes. Yet Giovani and Stewart show that E and F mistakes are inversely related i.e., attempts to reduce E-mistakes often can result in a larger number of F-mistakes. Therefore, human development as an objective would require to minimise the number of F-mistakes so as to ensure that all those entitled to benefits do in fact receive them. The presence of E and F mistakes has given rise to a controversy whether the welfare programmes should be broadly based or sharply focussed. While broadly based progammes are easier to manage, sharply focussed programmes become a necessity given the financial resources constraint faced by almost all countries.

An examination of the human development strategies pursued by different countries reveals the following lessons:

1. Countries which have accorded high priority to human capital formation have performed relatively better in terms of economic growth, employment, reduction in income inequalities and alleviation of poverty. This strategy has paid rich dividends in the case of newly industrialising countries.
2. When the distribution of income and assets is very uneven, high economic growth rates fail to translate themselves into enhanced standard of living of the people at large.
3. Well designed social expenditures by Government can significantly improve human development even when economic growth is low.

Share of Education in GNP

The share of education in GNP reflects the relative priority being accorded to education in the national economy. On the recommendation of the Education Commission (1966), the Government of India (1968) quantitatively targeted investing six per cent of national income in education from the public exchequer by 1986. As the goal has not been realised so far, it has repeatedly been reiterated that it will soon be fulfilled. The goal was set to be achieved by the end of the Ninth Five-Year Plan, i.e. by 2002.

Table 8.2: **Share of Education in GNP in India**

Year	*(Per cent)* *% of GNP*
1950-51	1.2
1960-70	2.8
1971-80	3.1
1981-90	3.2
1996-97* (R)	3.8
1997-98*	3.6

Presently 3.6 per cent of GNP is invested in education in India (1997-98). Compared to the very low level of 1.2 per cent in 1950-51, this marks very significant progress (Table—8.2). However, it needs to be underlined that this proportion is less than (i) the requirements of the education system to provide reasonable levels of quality education to all the students presently enrolled; (ii) the proportion of GNP invested in education in many other developing, leave alone developed, countries of the world, including Africa; and (iii) finally the proportion invested in India before the Jomtien conference. For instance, 4.9 per cent of Gross Domestic Product (GDP) was invested in education in India in 1990-1991. But ever since, it has been consistently declining. It should be noted that it would be stupendous the Ninth Five Year Plan, as promised by the government, from the current level of 3.6 per cent. Among the countries of the world on such data are available. India ranked 115th with respect to this indicator of national efforts on education, and amongst countries with a population of 100 million or more, India figures at the bottom, except Bangladesh.

Gender Budgeting

There are around 40 countries around the world that have followed the 1984 Australian Government initiative to look at governments' public expenditures and revenue collections from a gender point of view, that is, to assess the differential impact of such policies on women and girls as compared to men and boys. The most comprehensive experience is from South Africa that in

1995 started a gender audit exercise of all Ministries to identify inequalities and to take measures towards their elimination.

There are several aspects of gender budgeting. The collection of gender disaggregated data mentioned by the Finance Minister is one such aspect.

The actual allocations for women specific schemes or for the women's component in general schemes is important, as is the design of the schemes and programmes meant for women and children. Suppose for example that the Government of the day was to increase the allocations for women's training and skill development schemes but only for those that strengthened women's "traditional" roles as carers. More funds for Industrial Training Institutes to teach women how to sew and cook better, would hardly merit marks for gender sensitivity!

Another aspect is how general policies impact on women, collection of revenue, say through a hike in excise duties of essential commodities would certainly have a worse impact on women, because generally speaking in patriarchal cultures women would bear a disproportionately bigger share of the burden.

Thus is concept of gender budgeting if it is to be useful as a tool for women's advance has to be implemented in conjunction with an egalitarian and democratic vision.

In the light of global experience women's movements in India should be clear about their approach to gender budgeting. In the growing body of literature on gender budgeting or as it is more popularly called gender responsive budgets (GRBs) and its experience in different countries, the exercise is usually divorced from a critic of the mainstream macro-economic policy. It is usually seen as part of "gender mainstreaming" that is when the mainstream is taken as a given, written in stone. In its recent documents both the World Bank and the International Monetary Fund have commended the importance of GRBs. In the Poverty Reduction Strategy Papers prepared by the Bank and in the debt relief initiatives launched by the IMF in certain countries, the Bank-Fund panaceas have included "gender mainstreaming" and "GRBs" as practices, which are essential for "good governance". Mary Rusumbi the Director of the Tanzanian Institute working on gender budgeting in that country commented: "The support that the Government is getting from global institutions like the World Bank is very constraining. A lot of instructions come from them, which are kind of anti-progressive towards women and men. One such programme forced the Government to withdraw subsidies for small farmers, the great majority of whom are poor women. These policies are not analysed with a gender perspective."

Brinda Karat General Secretary All India Democratic Women's Association Says: The reference to gender budgeting in the Union Finance Minister, Chidambaram's speech brings into the parliamentary domain an issue that has been of concern to women's movements. While the speech is full of good intentions reflective of the Common Minimum Programme of the UPA, it is not backed up by the necessary funds thus impacting also on women specific schemes. Budget analysts have linked the low allocations to ideologies that promote privatization of social services and a retreat of the Government from its social responsibilities. Secondly, there is inadequate appreciation of the depth of the terrible conditions of distress of the rural poor, particularly women. Thus while the supposed financial restrictions have been used to explain the meagre allocations, say, for food-for-work schemes, such restrictions have not prevented the huge increase in Defence expenditures. The contrast with the rest of the allocations raise disturbing questions about the Government's priorities. Indeed in some cases they are directly discriminatory towards women.

REFERENCES

Mehta, M.M. (1976) *Human Resource in Development Planning*, New Delhi, Macmillan.

Vaidyanatha A. and P.R. Gopinathan Nair (eds.) 2001. *Elementary Education in Rural India*—A Grass Root View: Strategies in Human Development Sage, New Delhi.

Meir, Gerald M. (1984) *Leading Issues in Economic Development Delhi*. Oxford University Press.

Dutta Prabhat, *Major Issues in Development Debate Lessons in Empowerment from India*, Kanishka, New Delhi, 1988.

Articles

1. Rangarajan, C, Governor, Reserve Bank of India. Human Development and Economic Growth Convocation Address at the fifty-sixth convocation of Tata Institute of Social Science, Mumbai. University News, Month August 19, 1996, pp. 14-16 and 24.

2. Ponnambala Thiagrajan. A. Santhana Krishnan, S. Rajendran P., Human Capital formation University News, Mon, July 31, 1995, pp. 5-8.

3. Gupta, Vs. Social Sector Development and the Tenth Five Year Plan. Employment News. Vol. XXVII No. 1, 12 April 2002 pp. 1-2 and 7.

   Human Development and Enhancement of Quality of Life. Employment News 10—August 16, 2002.

4. Mohsin Ali Khan. Women's Education: Still a Distant Dream Yojana, Vol. 45, December 2001, pp. 20-43.

5. Singhal, D. Balika Shikshan Shivir: Datta S., An Effective Mode of Social Transformation. Yojana, Vol. 46, December 2002, pp. 35-36.

6. Raja Kutty, S. Primary Education in Rural Areas, Kurukshetra, Vol. 50, No. 12, Oct. 2002, pp. 11-20.

7. Ghosh B., Elementary Education as a Fundamental Rights—The Issues E.P.W., Dec. 13, 2001.

8. Rampal A., 2000 Education for Human Development in South Asia, E.P.W., July 22, 2000.

9. Ram Chandran V (2002) and Saihjee A., The New Segregatus Reflection on Gender and Equity in Primary Education in EPW April 27, 2002.

10. The Hindu. Right to Education a Distant Dream? 8 and 9 August 2002.

11. The Hindu. Gender Budgeting. July 24, 2004.

12. Agrawala, Bina (1995) Feminist Environmental of Ecofeminism, The Hindu Survey of Environment. pp. 1-14.

Kotvi, Ms. Empowerment of Women: Gender Equity-Amyth in Journal of Constitution and Parliamentary Studies. The Institute of Constitutional and Parliamentary Studies, New Delhi 1999. pp. 134-139.

9

Women Education and Development

Dr. Ashok Kumar Panda

Introduction

Man and Women both are the equally important part of the society. Beginning from the formation of the human society, man is recognised as the chief architect of the development. But actually his thought processor and action have been influenced by the genius is women so as to give proper shape to the social structure. Women is endowned with many virtues like beauty, grace, charm, softness, motherhood love and affection. All those wonderful qualities need self expression. Those qualities of the women can be helpful to develop the social, cultural and economic environment. Unfortunately "No country treats its women as well as its men." (Human Development Report 1993) There is a paradox here, which we must resolve. The sharp gender inequalities on one hand and continuing female infanticide on the other hand are the pointers to this reality. If we examine the root of a family, we reach the conclusion that she is mother. The best symbol of female values that has been created by the nature, mother is 'Creativity' and 'innovation' personified in solving human problem in the family. She represents excellence morality equality not in material terms but as a living cultural symbol practising these values. Out of all management experiences in business, industry, public service and society mother is the best manager nature has created. Mother's instinct has sustained mother India. In our country we can not deny the role of mother in the development of the family and the society. The UN has adopted 1994 as the year of the family with an emphasis that the family is the smallest democracy at the heart of the society. So unless the important manager of the family is educated how can we think the development of the nation.

The new technological developments have the potential impact in the lives of the women. We can seen how the access of the women to higher education has become easy. The same flexibilities are available in case of work also. But these facilities are not available in rural. So we have to create good environment to educate the 'mother culture'. This will help to us to develop in term of economy and culture. The chapter is to focus certain important factor which an educated women can contribute to the all round growth of the nation.

Population Stabilisation

Progress of a nation can be measured by the progress of its woman. All through the ages, women have contributed immensely to the enrichment of culture and progress of civilization. But they are not getting due recognition. It is only last couple of decades that there is growing awareness to improve the status and role of woman.

India's fertility rate and infants mortality rate have remained at very high levels primarily due to object poverty, widespread illiteracy particularly among the females. The impact of growing population on our economy is very serious. India at the time of independence had a population of 35 crore approximately and today it has crossed 100 crore. It causes over crowded urban slums, overstretching social service, school, health care, water and sanitation facility. It leads to increase unemployment, low wages and widened the gap between rich and poor. Women by their position biological otherwise, occupy a centre stage in relation to the population growth. The role of women is important in population stabilisation and family welfare. However, the relationship between education on the one hand and fertility and use of other contraceptive measures are interrelated. Educational status influences the socio-economic development of the family. Educational development works as a triggering mechanism to delay marriage and also limit the number of children. In India education has been found to be one of the most powerful indicators of fertility decline. It has been found that the total fertility rate of literate women is lower than that of illiterate women in rural area as well as in urban areas. Therefore, investment in education of women in fact is an investment in the success of programme leading to a reduction in population. So there is a need to ensure educational opportunities to the women with special incentives. The effect of cultural and economic bias require extra measures to develop the confidence among them.

Women Empowerment

The Tenth Plan (2002-2007) has made a major commitment towards "empowering women as the agent of socio-economic change and development." The Tenth plan suggests a three-fold strategy for empowering women through social, economic and gender justice. Empowerment of women in India is necessary to develop their status in the society. Over the years there has been slight increase in female population (407.1 million in 1991 and 495.7 million in 2001). The sex ratio is 927 in 1991 and 933 in 2001. Still there is a strong preference of male child in India. So social empowerment of women is a long and difficult process. It requires a change in the mindset of the people. Indian women get priority in education and health care.

Indian women are generally viewed as the burdens of the society. The contribution to their families are overlooked. To know the contribution of woman the work participation rate is considered as the suitable measure of economic role. The work participation rate is 19.7 per cent in 1981 to 25.7 per cent in 2001. This is very low than the male work participation.

Table 9.1: Very low than the Male Work Participation

(In per cent)

Census	*T/R/U*	*Female*	*Male*	*Persons*
1	*2*	*3*	*4*	*5*
1981	Total	19.7	52.6	36.7
	Rural	23.1	53.8	38.8
	Urban	8.3	49.1	30.0

(Table Contd...)

1	2	3	4	5
1991	Total	22.3	51.6	37.5
	Rural	26.5	52.5	40.1
	Urban	9.2	48.9	30.2
2001	Total	25.7	51.9	39.3
	Rural	31.0	52.4	42.0
	Urban	11.6	50.9	32.2

Source: Census of India: Government of India.

However in the unorganised sector women constitute 90 per cent of the total worker. Moreover, unskilled worker constitute 90 per cent of the rural and 70 per cent of the urban women workers. It is also important all the poor women, especially those below the poverty line have to perform the domestic duty and also supplement the family income.

If we observe the achievement of women in educational side it is remarkable, mainly in urban area. 1.25 lakh woman are graduate as doctors. It is 50 per cent of the total numbers. 50 per cent of the student who pass out every year in bachelor's degree in arts are girls. 21 per cent of India's software personnel and 25 per cent of engineering graduates are women. 77210 panchyats are headed by women, 13 number of women have been the Chief Minister of various states and 647 judges in 21 high courts after the independence (India Today, Women on 2005).

Women and the Career

Highly educated woman is concontrated in banking, IT, advertising, research and travel. These employ 20-35 per cent women of which 10.20 per cent are at the senior level. A study of 35 corporate done by cerebus consulting in 2002. The study found that 15-20 per cent female managers leave after getting married. On the rest 80-90 per cent exit after they have kids, despite 36 per cent of the companies providing tele-working option, where in the young mother could work from home. On the other hand they are successful in the career, due to the family support or from her maid. Behind every successful man there is a woman: behind every successful woman there is family support or support of a maid.

In rural area maximum women are doing something to contribute the family income. But their contribution and right are totally ignored by their own family. They are mainly working in the field of agriculture and mining. They are doing hardwork like man but getting less wages. This problem can be solved gradually if we educate the women to come forward.

Crime Against Women

The higher rate of crime is a matter of concern for the Home Ministry. Most of the crime are against women. On comparing the rate of total crime mainly six crimes are against the women. There are rape, kidnapping, dowry death, domestic violence, sexual harassment and mole station. It is also unfortunate that crime rate at Delhi is at least 150 per cent higher than any other state. It is a matter of grave concern. West Bengal is generally considered as one of the most progressive state with a tradition of better education. So crime against women is low.

Conclusion

It is clear from the above factors that women education is a vital point to develop a nation. At the same time the present education system can not help to solve all problems faced by the women in India. We must develop a value based education system which can aware the women of her duties and right. She will be allowed the full expression of her potential, so women can be dynamic partner in the building of new India. There are several Acts to save women from oppression like Child Marriage Act. The Special Marriage Act, Medical Termination of Pregnancy Act etc. But these Acts are not so helpful unless there is change of mindset of our society. This can is also achieve through the proper women education in the nation.

REFERENCES

1. Dogra Bharat, "*Woman Farm Workers Need to Organise them*", Yojana, Feb. 2002.
2. Ahluwalia Harjet, "*Empowerment of Women: An Economic Agenda*" Yojana, August 2000.
3. Heptulla, Najma, "*Role of Women in Population Stabilisation*" Yojana, August 2000.

4. Chattopadhyay, Arundhati, "*Women and Entrepreneurship*", Yojana, Jan. 2005.

5. Mission Possible, Business World 4th April, 2005.

6. Pradhan, Bibhuti B., "*Participation of Women in Economic Development of Manipur,*" Visim, Vol. XVII, No. 3, 4, page 66.

7. Mashelkar, R.A., "*The New Millennium A Five Point Indian Agenda*" Aryan Heritage, Dec. 99.

10

Development of Scheduled Caste Woman and Education

Dr. Suresh Kr. Sahu

Women constitute as large as 49.29 per cent of total population of Orissa and the development process, will be slow if such a large proportion population are not facilitated to participate. Further, it is noticed from various studies that the economic growth has been steady where the women are developed up to the mark and where they have not been allowed to be full participants in the process, the growth rate has been arrested at a particular stage. Education is a key to development. The main aim of education is to provide income generating skills and activities to rural women thereby bringing about a change in quality of life. Most of the studies conducted in developed and developing countries highlight that development of human capital through universal basic education has contributed significantly to economic growth. Again development economist as well as development planners are of opinion that literacy contributes to higher income to satisfy on the job and the possibility of unionization to protect the economic interest.

Bibek Debroy and Laveesh Bhandari, the two economists who developed the annual ranking of states for "India Today" decided to build an index of social progress for different states dividing them as "big states and small states." Orissa comes under "big state" category in the classification. According to them the position of Orissa in the education was 13th in 2003 and it came down to 14th in 2004. This indicates that the standard of general education is falling in Orissa.

As large as 93 types of schedule castes constitutes 16 per cent of total population of Orissa and there are about 8 per cent schedule caste women in the state. It is generally recognised that the schedule caste constitute a reasonable part of the population who are yet to reach the main stream in spite of all endeavours from the government level. To know whether a society is developed, under developed or developing it requires to understand the educational standard of the society. Because education plays an important role to determine the process of development in a society as well as in a country.

Education is an effective tool for upliftment of an individual and society as a whole. It helps for socio-economic development and personality development of the individuals. Education is essential for women to be able to participate and benefit from the growth process. Education can help them to enhance their literacy and provides better exposure to fight against poverty, exploitation, crime, discrimination, etc.

In the present study, an attempt has been made to highlight the educational standard and the work participation among the Bauris and Dhobas of two blocks namely Hinjlicut and Shergada of Ganjam district of Orissa.

Study Design

Data were collected from two blocks namely Hinjlicut and Shergada of Ganjam district of Orissa. A total of 114 Bauri households with 535 population and 100 Dhoba households with a population 511 have been covered through a structured schedule in two different surveys. The Bauris and the Dhobas are the two among the 93 schedule castes in the state of Orissa. Interview technique was mainly adopted for filling in the schedules. Observation technique particularly, non-participant type, was also followed as should be for any empirical study.

Orissa is accumulating consciousness in the field of education, which is also reflected among the backward women of the state. The educational status of population determines the level of development in a state. The spread of education among the schedule castes is gaining slow and continues moment due to the efforts of various agents. Development of education among the schedule castes, particularly among the schedule caste women is the least. It can be easily inferred from the data in the Table—10.1.

Table 10.1: Educational Standard Among the Study Population

Educational standard	*Bauri*		*Dhoba*		*Total*
	M	*F*	*M*	*F*	
Illiterate	119 (46.66)	171 (76)	74 (30.45)	108 (46.95)	472 (49.52)
Up to 5th	59 60 (23.13)	3 8 (16.88)	81 (33.33)	91 (39.56)	269 (28.22)
Up to 7th	35 (13.72)	10 (4.44)	32 (13.16)	20 (08.69)	97 (10.17)
Up to 10th	30 (11.76)	06 (2.66)	46 (18.93)	08 (03.48)	90 (9.44)
Above 10th	12 (4.70)	–	10 (04.11)	03 (01.30)	25 (2.62)
Total Literacy	136 (53.33)	54 (24)	169 (69.54)	122 (53.04)	481 (50.47)
Total Population	255 (100)	225 (100)	243 (100)	230 (100)	953 (100)

Children below the age of 5 years are excluded.

The above table depicts the percentage of literates among Bauri male is 53 per cent and female is 24 per cent and among Dhoba male is 69 per cent and female is 53 per cent whereas the total literate male in Orissa is 75.95 per cent and 50.95 per cent for females (census 2001). Further it is found that the male literacy among Dhoba population is ahead of the state literacy.

The Literate percentage between Bauri and Dhoba females are 76 per cent and 47 per cent respectively. Interestingly 1.30 Dhoba female crossed 10th standard but no female among Bauris has reached up to that level.

It is found from the data that the Dhobas are comparatively developed in education from the Bauris. It may be due to the availability of education institutes in the area, better exposure and because of demonstration effect.

The occupations are hereditary as per the caste system in India. But towards the last century the position has changed considerably. Ghurye (1961) in his book "caste and occupation" rightly observed that there was no freedom of occupation among the larger number of castes. The members of the backward classes are unable to look upon the future of their children as something, which could be superior to what has been their lot. When the sweeper and the barber have been brought up in a tradition which makes them feel that to serve the society in the same occupation is "dharma" and to break away from it is "adharma", it is not possible to expect any kind of response, (Kuppuswamy, 2000).

Education and improvement in education system also brings about change in society, but the education network should be desired to bring about a social change particularly in occupation. Education acts as an agent of social change and with proper education, a man develops a middle class attitude, irrespective of the class from which he hails.

The occupational changes can be valued, considering the above facts, as the effect of educational among Bauris and Dhobas of the study population from the Table—10.2.

Table 10.2: Distribution of Economic Active Population in the Study Area

Name of the occupation	*Bauri*		*Dhoba*		*Total*
	Male	*Female*	*Male*	*Female*	
1	2	3	4	5	6
Cultivation	24 (8.57)	24 (9.41)	05 (1.90)	–	53 (5.06)
Wage earner	82 (29.28)	119 (46.66)	104 (39.54)	47 (18.95)	352 (33.65)
Government service	03 (1.07)	–	04 (1.52)	–	07 (0.66)
Private service	21 (7.5)	03 (1.17)	15 (5.70)	–	39 (3.72)
Business	02 (0.71)	–	11 (4.18)	–	13 (1.24)

(Table Contd...)

1	2	3	4	5	6
Tailor	–	–	04 (1.52)	01 (0.40)	05 (0.47)
Tractor driver	03 (1.07)	–	–	–	03 (0.28)
Rickshaw puller	30 (10.71)	–	12 (4.56)	–	42 (4.01)
Cloth washer	–	–	26 (9.88)	94 (37.90)	120 (11.47)
Missionary work	02 (0.79)	–	–	–	02 (0.19)
Total Worker	167 (59.64)	146 (57.25)	181 (68.83)	142 (57.26)	636 (60.80)
Total population	280 (100)	255 (100)	263 (100)	248 (100)	1046 (100)

The above table depicts that about 60 per cent males and 57 per cent females among the Bauris and about 69 per cent males and 57 per cent females among the Dhoba population are engaged in different economic activities. Interestingly 57 per cent women in both sections of population are engaged in different economic activities.

Even though there are reservations for schedule caste people in the different government services, only 1.07 per cent Bauri males and 1.52 per cent Dhoba males are in government service but surprisingly it is found no women from both the sections are employed in the government offices. Further, it is also found that the Dhoba population, of the study area, diverted from their traditional occupation and accepted different occupations because of the educational development. The Bauri population of the study area is also noticed occupational change only because of the educational standard.

The study shows that schedule caste women are lagging behind from their counterpart women in the main stream of course the Dhoba women are comparatively developed. It indicates that when women are educated their dependence automatically disappears or at least decreases. Education increases women's awareness and leads to their overall development thereby helps the nation to develop. Hence it is said, "If you educate a man you educate an individual and if you educate a woman, you educate a family."

After the 58 years of independence the social and occupational change found in the meager population of the study area, is not up to the mark. Of course the Government has left no stone unturned for the all-round development of the schedule castes in India. The constitution prescribes protection and safeguards the schedule castes by promoting their educational and economic interest. Fur the upliftment of the schedule castes the Government has taken so many steps such as set up of three parliamentary committees in 1961, 1971, and 1973, formed welfare department in different states and also allowed different voluntary organisations to promote welfare of the schedule castes. Not only that the Government but also started different schemes such as coaching and allied schemes, book bank schemes Pre-Matric and Post-Matric scholarships only for their [S.Cs] educational development. There is also provision of reservation of seats for the schedule castes in different educational institutes, still than, why these people are lagging far behind the main stream, especially the schedule caste woman? To find out the answer further research is required.

The scourge of illiteracy can be eliminated from Orissa through a special provision for schedule caste woman in education policy and their honest implementation. In view of the above facts, we can conclude that economic development of a country, is not possible at all without the elevation of the status of woman. Moreover the status of woman can be elevated only when they are made free from economic, social and psychological chains through proper education and training.

REFERENCES

Debroy, Bibek and Bhandari Laveesh (2004), *Indias Best and Worst*, (Annual Ranking of States) India Today, Delhi.

Ghurya, G.S. (2000), *Caste and Race in India*, Popular Prakashan, Bombay–34.

Ghurya, G.S. (1961), *Caste and Occupation*, Popular Prakashan, Bombay–34.

Hutton, J.H (1946), *Caste in India*, Oxford University Press.

Kuppuswamy, B (2000), *Social Change in India*, Konark Publishers Pvt. Ltd. Delhi–92.

Sing, Soran, (1987), *Schedule Castes of India Dimensions of Social Change*, Gian Publishing House, Delhi.

11

Education to Challenge Women Oppression

Prof. Devdutta Choudhury

Women at home and abroad are considered weaker, oppressed, marginalised, disadvantaged, exploited, harassed, victimized to environmental degradation, excluded from decision-making process trapped in occupational segregations. Lifelong discriminations have increased their oppression and made them to suffer to suffer from Triple unjusts. Excess workload, no/less wage no status. Women involvement recognised as only casual, supplementary and supporting. The lack of visibility of her work in the eyes of her family and society is one of the vital aspect of women oppressions.

Mr. Reedy (1994) says "although women constitute 50 per cent of population, perform 2/3 work and produce 50 per cent of food consumed by the Indians, they earn only 1/3 of the remunerations and 10 per cent of property of the country."[1]

UNO study group has remarked "women earn only 10 per cent of worlds income and own less then 10 per cent of its property... Of 1.3 billion people living in absolute poverty today over 900 millions are women."[2]

Women in India are oppressed inside home, in the workplace due to gender bias. Violence against women, her work participation, less political involvement are few important indicators of her lower social status and oppressions.

Violence Against Women

Women's identity, self-esteem, psychological and emotional health are undermined by physical violence, sexual, psychological and emotional abuses, forced child marriages, restrictions on her mobility, over work, threats and verbal abuses.[3]

Important forms of violences are beating by angry and drunk husbands, dowry torches leading to death, rape, molestations etc. One in every four girls and one in seven boys in the world are sexually abused. In India one in every 10 children is sexually abused.[4]

The Annual report—2002 of National Crime Records Bureau (NCRB) reveals that crime against women has increased by 2.7 per cent during the year 2001-2002 in India. Rape cases with child victims has increased by 20 per cent in 2002. The crime rate was highest in Delhi.[5]

Further female feticide and infanticide account for a larger amount of violences against women. Parents prefer spending Rs. 500 now in female feticide to the expenditure of lakhs of rupees twenty years after.

Thus women have been victims of different types of violences at all levels in all age groups.

Women Work—Participation

Women of developed nations are more engaged in secondary and service sectors and lesser in primary sector compared to the woman work participation in developing nations due to their higher education content and skill possession. The illiterate, unskilled women of developing nations like India have no choice but to join the primary sector for earning their bread at a lower wage rate. Statistics on woman work—participation in different countries mentioned below, support to this observation.

Table 11.1: Female Work—Participation (2002) in Per cent Countries Primary Sector Secondary Sector Service Sector

Australia	3	10	87
U.S.A.	1	12	87
U.K.	1	11	88
Sri Lanka	49	22	29
Bangladesh	77	9	14
India	60	15	25

Source: ILO-2002, used women's Link vol. 10/4 of 2004.

The following inferences can be drawn from Table—11.1.

(a) The women work force in Australia, USA, UK are more engaged in service sector and very lesser (1 per cent to 3 per cent) in primary sector.

(b) The women work-participation in India is higher in primary sector and lesser in secondary and service sectors.

Further studies of ILO indicate that women are under-represented at the highest levels of the occupational hierarchy in all parts of the globe. It is 11 per cent in USA, 1.5 per cent in Germany, 8 per cent in Spain, 9 per cent in Japan, 17 per cent in Sri Lanka and 8 per cent in India.[6]

Table 11.2: Women and Their Participation in Politics

Countries	*Year of voting right*	*Year to stand for election*	*% of seats in the parliament held by women*	
			Lower House	*Upper House*
Australia	1962	1962	25.3	28.9
USA	1960	–	14.3	13
UK	1928	1928	17.9	16.7
Sri Lanka	1931	1931	44	–
India	1950	1950	8.8	10.3
Bangladesh	1972	1972	2	–

Source: Women's Link vol. 10/4 of 2004.

Table—11.2 indicate that:

(i) Political participation of women in Australia, USA, UK is not only older but also higher in magnitude compared to the developing nations like India, Bangladesh.

(ii) Percentage of seats in parliament held by women in Sri Lanka is greater than the developed nations.

Though Indian women leaders are selected to parliament around 19 per cent to both the houses, they are more encouraged constitutionally to take part in the local-self govt. after the enactment of the 73rd and 74th amendment of the constitution in the year 1992.

But the women-pradhans as Sarpanch, Chairpersons, Samiti-members prove to be less effective due to their illiteracy. They are substituted by their husbands/old male Pradhans to act in their office on their behalf there by making themselves de-jury in their offices.

A study in Haryana on the topic "women in local governance has revealed "21 per cent of women representatives studied up to primary level, 17 per cent got education up to high school level. Only two of them were graduates. Low level of education of women representatives became stumbling block in the way of their taking of the responsibilities in panchayats.[7]

Education of Women is a Challenge for Women Oppression

Women of developing nations particularly in India are more oppressed in the field of work-participation, prone to several forms of violences due to their illiteracy and ignorance. They have failed to present their problems at the national level due to their less representation in national politics. Such oppression and depressions can be minimised by educating the girl-child and women. But Govt. of India has listed education in the state list by providing a minimum of only 3 per cent of the union budget allocations. In Orissa the allocations for education in the state budget has been reduced from 21 per cent to 8 per cent now. Low budgetary allocation for education in the union and state budget has reduced the scope for the rural students to go for higher education.

Of course the govt. records reveal that literacy rate in India has increased by more than the six times during the period 1951-2001 as shown below in Table—11.3.

Table 11.3: Literacy Rate in India

Year	*Male (%)*	*Female (%)*
1951	27.16	8.86
1961	40.40	15.35
1971	45.96	21.97
1981	56.38	29.76
1991	64.13	39.29
2000	75.85	54.16

Source: Census of India 2001.

Degree of literacy has increased in India. But the women literacy is not yet at par with the male literacy rate. The gap between male and female literacy is still significant. More over literacy status is mere a beginning to enter into the world of knowledge. A large number of girl child and women (46 per cent) are still illiterate and powerless due to their poverty and illiteracy.

The women of India should be provided with upgrade technical skills to generate income from their self-employed projects. Some of the priority areas where the rural women are to be sensitised and given training are: *water, health, nutrition, agriculture, legal awareness*.

1. The technique of harvesting rainwater for drinking and irrigation purposes should be taught to the rural women.
2. They should be taught to grow in their back yards green for iron, curry leaves for vitamins, mushrooms for protein.
3. They must be trained to prepare bio-fertilisers.
4. Vocational educational must be imparted to use local resources to earn money-income.

The entire success of the family and nation depends on the women at home and work place. Education (formal, informal, vocational) is of immense importance to reduce women oppression. The govt. at the centre and state level should allocate more resources for the empowerment of women through more education, vocational training programmes. The empowered women should be serious in making right efforts to make free their fellow sisters from gender exploitation and man-made oppressions also.

REFERENCES

1. *Kurukhtra* Vol. XL 11/12 – 1994.
2. The World of Works No. 19-1997.
3. *Women's Link* – Editorial Vol. 10/4 – 2004.
4. *W.H.O. Report* – 2004.
5. *I.L.O. Report* – 2004.
6. *Women's Link* Vol. 10/4 – 2004.
7. *Yojana*, December 2003.

Index